Bluebirds Reunited

The Fall and Rise of Cardiff City

Aled Blake

ST DAVID'S PRESS

Cardiff

Published in Wales by St. David's Press, an imprint of

Ashley Drake Publishing Ltd
PO Box 733
Cardiff
CF14 7ZY

www.st-davids-press.wales

First Impression – 2018

ISBN
Paperback: 978-1-902719-757

British Library Cataloguing-in-Publication Data.
A CIP catalogue for this book is available from the British Library.

Typeset by Prepress Plus, India (www.prepressplus.in)
Printed in the Czech Republic by Akcent Media.
Cover design by Siôn Ilar, Welsh Books Council, Aberystwyth.
Cover images © Wales News.

Contents

For Ossie

Foreword

Following Cardiff City's road to the Premier League has been a privilege and a thrill.

This is the amazing story of what it's really taken for Neil Warnock to bring a bruised club from the bottom of the league to the top of the Championship. It explores how Warnock used grit, skilful man-management and fan power, to unite the dressing room and the stands for the first time in years – creating a team everyone wants to be a part of. Playing for Cardiff City was a great honour for me, and I've been so proud watching from the press box as Warnock breathed a new fire into the club.

Aled Blake examines in detail how the manager transformed its fortunes with a modest budget, when it felt like many people had given up on City's dream. Bluebirds' supporters have had a tough ride, and Aled lets them speak in their own words about the disappointments and the highs, and the impact of the Warnock Way on their club.

Via fan interviews, insider knowledge and interviews with the man himself, this book tracks a fascinating timeline, unpicking every moment that counted in a promotion season where everything changed.

Danny Gabbidon
July 2018

Acknowledgements

It takes a team of friends and family to write a book. I didn't realise that until now, so some thanks are in order.

First, to Ashley Drake of St. David's Press for showing the confidence in me and my idea from the very start and allowing me to write a book about my life's passion. To Neil Warnock, not only for everything he's done for Cardiff City, but for phoning me back and giving me his time when many others in his profession would probably have ignored me ("All right, son? I'm just driving onto a ferry right now."). He is the manager we deserve.

To Dom Booth at *WalesOnline*, for his time. BBC Wales' Chris Wathan, meanwhile, has been a trusted mentor. Cheers Chris. To Salvatore Vara at the brilliant Calabrisella for proving multiculturalism works and being at the heart of the promotion celebrations. To all the fans I spoke to: James Leighton, Sarah McCreadie, Keith Morgan, Philip Nifield, my old F Block compatriots and friends, Dan Tyte and David Owens (that vegan beer is on its way to you), Siân Matheson, Gordon Goldsmith and many more who I've not been able to name here.

To Paul Rowland for his encouragement and loyal friendship, and without whom I would never have had this chance. I could not have got through the more difficult moments without the moral support of Steffan Rhys, Jonathan Morgan and Marc Jennings. I'm indebted also to Robin Wilkinson for his patient editing work and morale boosting words.

I'd like to thank Marc and Beth as well as my brother and sister, Rhys and Nia, along with Claire and Paul, for looking after Joseph when we needed people to step in and time was short: sticky rice. To Clive for the babysitting and City chats, and Mari and John, as ever, for the free Mondays – you're all on the IOU list. I want to say thank you Mum and Dad, not just for the childcare, but Dad: for infecting me with my unshakeable love of Cardiff City (a blessing and a curse) and letting it take over my life (for too many years); and Mum: for giving me a pleasure in words which has stuck with me. Thank you for fostering my passions.

Finally, words cannot express the gratitude I have to my wife, Claire: my fiercest critic and most supportive friend through all this. She's been a constant sounding board for even the most minor of quibbles. Claire, your sacrifices are never unappreciated and always cherished. You are the kick up the bum I need.

Introduction

The life of a Cardiff City supporter is never easy. Keeping up with football's longest-running soap opera means that sometimes you can be forgiven for forgetting about what's actually happening on the field. You could also argue everything that comes with being a Bluebird makes the experience more thrilling. The love, the hate, the disappointment and the jubilation. It's all what you sign up for when you become a City fan.

That's probably why Neil Warnock became such a popular manager at the Cardiff City Stadium. The promotion to the Premier League which he masterminded from the moment he joined in October 2016 was one like no other in the club's history. It's unlikely it'll ever be replicated by anyone else.

- What made it so memorable?
- How was Warnock able to unite such a fractured club?
- How did underrated Cardiff City manage to pip big-spending Aston Villa and glamorous Fulham to automatic promotion?
- Has there ever been a City squad of players as hard-working and committed as this one?

It's a story with many parts and one which doesn't really begin with Warnock at all, but with City's last foray into the top division in English football. The drama which had gone before provided the foundations for Warnock's extraordinary 18 months. Cardiff City was a club made for him in a time when it was ripe for his magic touch.

Times like this are rare for a football fan. They're rarer still for a City supporter. We've had success in the last couple of decades, there've been good times – trips to Wembley (where we mostly lost), promotion battles (perennial under Dave Jones in the Championship) and dramatic victories in extraordinary circumstances (that famous FA Cup win against Leeds Utd at Ninian Park), and of course that first season we went up to the Premier League in 2013.

There've been plenty of bad times too. Strange that among the best, and maybe worst, was the 2012-13 Championship winning season. I still well remember the weird feeling that Tuesday night in April when a 0-0 draw against Charlton secured our promotion. There was something jarring, deep down it felt wrong watching a Cardiff City team playing in red and winning lots of matches. The winning was great, but who knew that the change of colour would matter so much emotionally? Plenty will say they did.

I tried to be a pragmatist, for what was the alternative (was there an alternative at all?), but couldn't escape a lingering feeling of discomfort. You might even call it guilt. I think many fans felt the same. Others were turned off altogether.

While there was an exuberance at that success, and wonderful as it was to see the club back where we thought it belonged (ah, the arrogance of being a City fan), there was an artificiality to it too which resonated well beyond the summer of 2013. Splits between fans themselves, between supporters and club, opened up. Since then so much has happened.

Ultimately, you can't fail to appreciate the work the club has done in rebuilding a connection with supporters, and understanding that you have nothing if you don't have unity and identity. It has, though, been the down-to-earth, straightforward Neil Warnock who has been the final, crucial piece in re-establishing that bond.

The last 18 months have been thrilling. The football has had a blood-and-thunder quality to it which City fans find endearing. Warnock has been that newness that was needed at the Cardiff City Stadium. Neil Warnock: right man, right club, right time. You could not have hoped for a more serendipitous appointment. You could not have dreamed of a better season to be a Bluebird again. Who knows what this club can achieve in the Premier League?

1

A Siege Mentality

"We've been kicked up and down, written off many times and we've come back and surprised everyone in the league."

Neil Warnock

It may be that footballers don't realise, understand or even care about the impact they have on people's lives. Their mistakes, their moments of brilliance, their highs and lows, goals, tackles, misses and saves really do have tangible emotional effects on the people who get so tied up in the results of their team. Some much more than others.

Natasha Murphy had taken her son Dylan Pugh to be a part of the celebration parade on a scorching hot day in May 2018, the week after promotion was won. Her words tell so much about what supporting Cardiff City means for people – football at its most egalitarian is football at its best.

"Dylan is autistic and the only thing he cares about is Cardiff City," she told *WalesOnline*. "For him to come here and experience it and see his idols is the best thing that could happen. He was two last time."

What it must mean to be able to provide such joy to someone you might not even know exists. It's one of the many beautiful things about football. At the parade, Dylan and thousands of others were turning the city into a giddy, blue carnival. Two open-top buses were escorted from the stadium to Cardiff Castle, via Cowbridge Road, where a fiesta had spontaneously begun.

"One team in Wales, there's only one team in Wales," the supporters sang as the convoy moved slowly on. The buses were visibly bouncing as just about everyone at the club who'd had a hand in the season's success – from players, to admin staff, to the key members of the coaching team – travelled joyously towards Cardiff Castle.

It was the club's second promotion to the Premier League, but this one felt different. Even if the Bluebirds only spend one season in the top division, fans know they'll enjoy it more than last time.

"One Neil Warnock, there's only one Neil Warnock," roared the crowd as the buses edged slowly along Castle Street.

The podium was ready. The crowd was wound up. Players and staff began to step on. Someone climbs the traffic lights on Castle Street, holding a Welsh flag in blue, yellow and white, while a teenage girl watching the big screen from someone's sunburned shoulders launches smoke flares into the sky. Then Neil Warnock takes centre stage, holding his promotion trophy before swapping it for the microphone. He's about to tell everyone what he thinks about leading another team to another promotion.

In the shadow of the castle – a legacy of the city's Victorian industrial supremacy – this rugged northerner, whose life has been shaped growing up in the grinding poverty of steel city Sheffield, is revelling in proving everyone wrong.

Football's perennial underdog has beaten the odds again. How has he done it? What's his inspiration? Where does he find the energy? Men half his age couldn't do it, but a tireless

69-year-old has turned Cardiff City from Championship also-rans into a Premier League club.

Thousands throng the city centre on this humid Sunday afternoon in the middle of May – cancelling plans for barbecues and beer gardens. A giant flag, as wide as four car lanes, has made it through the streets of nearby Canton and is providing shelter from the heat to a group who've travelled with this convoy of joy.

The party's guest of honour is up. Warnock's ready to speak.

"Not one of you lot thought we would get promotion this season," he bristles.

The cheering, if forgetful, City supporters claim otherwise.

"No, not one of you – don't you lie!"

It's said with some jest, but Warnock means it.

He's just thanked his chairman, Mehmet Dalman, and chief executive, Ken Choo, for their support in getting the club out of the Championship, but it's his opening message to the fans which sheds light on both a dressing room brought together by, and a team spirit built on, a siege mentality – everyone is against us: even, at times, our own fans.

There's a twinkle in his eye as he talks, but Warnock is making an important point to his players here as much as he is to the cheering supporters. Even now, amid historic celebrations, the mercurial Yorkshireman is using all his man-management experience to send everyone who's listening – from the fans before him, to his beaming chief executive, to the players on the stage behind – a message.

"We, the underdogs, succeeded. Nobody believed we could, or would, and we can and will succeed again."

He continues his speech. After delivering his message to the players he knows how to make fans feel great about themselves: "Days like today make us realise how big we are, especially in Wales. You have to be our 12th man next year. That Reading game last week I have never heard a crowd as noisy as that in my life."

For Warnock, it wasn't just enough to come in and save Cardiff City from what looked like almost certain relegation to League One the season before. He knew he wouldn't be here for an easy ride.

He loves the Championship and he loves winning. It seems as though he loves life at Cardiff City too.

No, this wasn't merely about stopping a club from going down. Warnock wanted another promotion.

Relaxing into his speech now, he becomes more mischievous. "What I would like to say lads is, I've got my eighth promotion but I've never been in Europe yet. So how many will say 'no chance'? It's a great, great feeling at the moment. All the lads have had to put up with a few rollickings throughout the season. We've been kicked up and down, written off many times and we've come back and surprised everyone in the league. I've got to say a massive thank you to these guys behind me."

He is, of course, referring to the squad. Once a ragtag bunch of rejects, write-offs and never-could-have-beens who are now one of the most popular sides in Cardiff's history. When he took control of the club, some of his now key men weren't even playing, others were on the bench. Arguably the star man of the Warnock era – the Danish striker Kenneth Zohore – was a figure of fun among fans, who ridiculed the player on social media and internet forums so bereft was he of confidence and, it seemed, ability.

"One of the worst players I've seen in a City shirt," wrote Blue blood on the CCMB forum in September 2016 after a home defeat to Derby County. On the same thread, Neathblue63 said: "Worst Cardiff striker I have seen in my 40 years supporting. Offers absolutely nothing, one paced (slow), can't win a header, how he got a pro contract is seriously baffling...Bruno was better up front, shocking."

CCMB user islandblue replied: "Just been trying to remember if I've seen any worse strikers playing for City over the years, even in the dungeon years of the mid 80s. Even past greats such as Morris Scott, Tony Philiskirk and Graham Withey were a level above Zohore tonight."

A few months later, by the end of Warnock's first season at the club, he was the Bluebirds' most prized asset, one of the most sought-after players outside the Premier League and the subject of bids from Brighton rumoured to have beeen around £15m.

The secret to this almost unbelievable transformation? A word in his ear from Warnock, who – lacking in options one December Saturday afternoon – took a gamble on him in a match against Wolverhampton Wanderers and threw him on from the bench.

This was not the Kenneth Zohore Cardiff fans had seen before. It was a Zohore with pace and desire; a Zohore who was running at defenders and chasing down lost causes. He had gone from "disgrace" (Warnock's own words about the player) to the first name on his team sheet.

"He was a disgrace. He was strutting about the place and he didn't push himself," the City manager told Sky Sports' *Goals on Sunday*. "We played Wolves at home and we were losing 1-0 at half time. And there was nothing on the bench, only him. So I pulled him into the bathroom and said 'I'm going to put you on now'. In a few words that I can't really say in the morning, I said, 'This is your career son, you can either go to Belgium or you can show me what you can do'. And he's never looked back. He's worked his socks off. He can be even better. He's got all the attributes, he just needed to work."

It is a telling vignette of life in a Warnock side. A player can be given all the world class coaching in the world, but ultimately, success comes down to an individual's motivation to perform, and to perform at their very best. Warnock understands this, and how to do it, more than most.

Warnock hasn't just transformed the players, though, he has transformed a club. He gets south Wales, the valley communities, the city of Cardiff, the Bluebirds and the supporters, who he's described as, "My kind of fans, my kind of people". Even the club's marketing department has keyed into the Warnock way of thinking, using his motto to entice ticket sales and cultivate the new feeling of togetherness at the club.

He's a tough Yorkshireman, who grew up in a hard-working family in Sheffield. His mother had multiple sclerosis and died when he was 13, while his dad worked long shifts in the city's famous steel industry. Yorkshire is not so different, culturally, from industrial south Wales – as he has pointed out himself. It's been clear from the start of his time at the club that Warnock, so proudly working class himself, has an intuitive understanding of the Cardiff City fan. He's put in hours of his own time working to reconnect what was an obviously broken club with its fans, attending forums and events at sports and social clubs across the valleys.

Appreciating Warnock's own background (he was born in a house on the halfway line of a football pitch) and the work he put in to carve out a career as a lower league footballer of limited ability, provides context for both his affiliation with the people in Cardiff City's ex-industrial hinterland and his desire to succeed in the face of adversity.

"As a manager, I've wanted to prove – usually – chairmen wrong," he told BBC Wales' Daniel Davies in a characteristically blunt interview for *Wales Live*. He admits he carries a chip on his shoulder, a suspicion towards authority and power, and it's this which has helped give him such drive through his career. It might also explain his constant run-ins with referees, opposition managers, supporters and players.

"Love me or loathe me, I've always been the type of bloke people have had an opinion about," Warnock writes in his autobiography *Made in Sheffield*. "And I've made a habit of picking myself up when I've been knocked down. I haven't had it easy in football. I've spent a lot of time in the lower divisions, grafting and scraping. I've worked and worked and worked to get to the top."

Such drive to succeed does not come without its victims. Down the years, Warnock has managed to fall out with just about everyone and everything in football, and Cardiff City fans love him for it. His drive has made him one of the most divisive figures in the game, someone who has a habit of telling others exactly what they don't want to hear. Yep, that suits the Bluebirds down to the ground, too.

"I've either [fallen] out with the chairman or they've not supported me," he said. "If they've not supported me or they've told me lies then I've not suffered fools gladly. I want to show them, 'you should've had me, pal'."

Is it any wonder Warnock has been such a good fit at Cardiff City? Bluebirds supporters have rarely demanded teams play their football patiently and skilfully. There are more cheers at the Cardiff City Stadium for a forward chasing down defenders, or a full-throttled tackle from a committed midfielder than would be for a deft flick, neat touch or cute pass. That's not to say these fans aren't educated about football and how it could and should, so the pundits tell us, be played.

They enjoy watching flowing football – Dave Jones' five years in charge of the club saw talents such as Jay Bothroyd, Michael Chopra and Jason Koumas outplay opposition teams match after match and supporters loved it. It's simply that, like Warnock, they're pragmatic about success and how it comes. They want to see players with heart and commitment – defenders like Sol Bamba who'd put his body in front of shots flying towards the goal. They're loyal to players who share their passion for the club and for winning matches. Attractive football means little if you can't win a game.

Warnock, direct (maybe) in football and direct (definitely) in manner, fitted perfectly with a supporter base crying out for someone to bring a bit of passion back to Cardiff, and he did that in spades. The result? A record eighth promotion and thousands of adoring Cardiff City fans lining the streets of the capital, cheering on his never-say-die squad of players – "like looking after 25 kids", says Warnock.

He understands that dynamic better than anyone. In an interview for the job at Norwich, Warnock enjoys recounting, he was asked if he thought fans would enjoy seeing their team playing the Warnock Way. "What, winning?" he responded. Carrow Road wasn't for him.

At former club Queens Park Rangers, Warnock gave the skilful Adel Tarrabt the captain's armband, explaining to senior players – more conventional captain material – that it was up to them to keep up morale when times would get tough, but giving Tarrabt the captaincy proved the masterstroke in his success at QPR. Hardly a typical Warnock player – with all his guile came as much egotistical baggage – but he was the standout player of that Rangers team which won promotion to the Premier League. The senior players rallied, Tarrabt was made to feel like a superstar and it worked.

At Cardiff City, it's been Kenneth Zohore who's been the wasted talent to have been given a career U-turn thanks to Warnock's stardust. Around that has been built that siege mentality which Warnock is so adept at fashioning. Is it any coincidence that promotion was clinched in a 0-0 draw at home against Reading? No frills, but the job was done.

Above it all, Warnock kept up the pretence that his squad had no right to be where they were – and that nobody, apart from him and his players, believed they would do something special. It kept a sense of perspective and reality at the club, there was never going to be any celebrating too soon, any talk of promotion, any thoughts of Premier League football, until it suited Warnock's psychological strategy.

To the BBC's Dan Davies again: "The way that I am, there is going to be quite a lot of joy when I'm a failure because everybody loves to knock me, but it just drives me on. Like the season that's just gone, there has been periods where a lot of the media, and our fans as well, thought we had blown it. That's where I've earned my money this year."

Fulham buckled under the pressure to get the win they needed in their last match – and Neil Warnock's Cardiff City did just enough. This was a Championship promotion race very different to most before it. In any other year, Cardiff or Fulham would have walked the division with the points they'd accumulated.

When City won the division in 2013 they had 87 points and were up by April having picked up the points they needed in the most unassuming of ways. Fulham, in 2018, with flowing football and attacking flair, had amassed 88 points after the last match of the season.

Somehow, Cardiff City ground out 90 points, had a record-breaking start to the season, enjoyed a winning run of eight matches after the New Year, and still could not come top of the table, lagging behind Nuno Espírito Santo's unstoppable Wolves side.

Fulham had gone on a mind-boggling unbeaten run, and up until that crucial final game of the season at Birmingham City, they had not lost a league match in 2018. It was the best record in English football, but it wasn't good enough to take the place of Cardiff City. Manager Slaviša Jokanović described it as "incredible but it's not important", merely "an interesting statistical detail" in the twists and turns of a dramatic promotion chase where your main rival is a Neil Warnock-led side who just will not go away.

That must have been annoying, though Jakanović – who eventually led his side to a deserved promotion via the play-offs – would never have dared to admit it. "We have improved greatly in these past months though; we have shown the character to go and win games," Jakanović told journalists before the season finale. "I don't know why we would change now. We have played many finals in the last few months, it's another final for us and there's a possibility we might have another two or three finals after this."

He'd already predicted Cardiff – needing to match or better Fulham's result at Birmingham on the final day to secure second spot in the league – would drop points against Reading. Jokanović was proved right, of course, but he didn't foresee his team being beaten 3-1 by a relegation-threatened Birmingham City.

Fulham, the glamorous upmarket team who played enviably sharp football, became the focus for the nearby London-based media now paying attention (as they invariably do, come the end of the season) to the Championship promotion story, which totally suited Warnock and his wily coaching team of Kevin Blackwell and Ronnie Jepson.

Speaking ahead of the forgettable, rearranged Derby game in April as the season drew to a close, Warnock spoke of Fulham glowingly. Praising them helped put into context his own side's colossal achievement. "In a normal season, Fulham would have walked it by now. Twenty-two games unbeaten with the players they've got," Warnock said. "We must be like something they want to swat away, like a rash or something, but we keep going and it's making it an interesting end to the season for TV and the media because otherwise it would just be a two-horse race and it would have been finished by now."

Both Jakanović and Warnock had tried during these last weeks to pile pressure on the other side, to make their rivals' fans the more jittery. If they could sense any leg wobbles in their opponent's ranks, they'd exploit it. Knowing that your rivals are human, with human frailties, is important to remember in these situations. Managing stress is a crucial skill during such fraught times.

It was Warnock, an expert in psychology, who was winner in the mind-games even as City began to show signs of their own slip-ups. He revelled in the mental tit-for-tats (you can see the pleasure he takes in them during press conferences).

Jakanović opens: The situation is now in Cardiff's control.

Warnock bats back: We're the hunters again, not the hunted, and we love it.

Jakanović: I'm not thinking about finishing second.

Warnock: That Fulham squad is full of good pros, they deserve to go up.

Jakanović: Honestly, we didn't even think we'd get this far, this record run we're on is meaningless.

Warnock: I bet Fulham wish we weren't here.

Pressure, pressure, pressure. Warnock knows how to keep his rivals in a constant state of it, and how to shield his own players and fans. It was, in the end, Fulham who buckled so dramatically and Cardiff who endured, who did what they'd done all season: just enough to get over the line. Just enough is enough and promotion was won.

In his press conference after that Reading game, Warnock put into perspective how enormous an achievement this promotion was for him personally. "It seems such a long time ago [when he arrived at Cardiff City], the state the club was in.

I've seen the fans today on the pitch, a full house, the owners and everyone together, it's got to be the best ever job I've done in my life."

The old football clichés about Warnock are usually true. You know the ones – he's seen it all and done it all, a proper football man, in the results business he makes a profit – yet to have already won seven promotions in a career as a manager is an achievement most colleagues in his profession will never be able to emulate.

Most of those promotions had elements of luck, stories of dogmatic determination and periods where questions were asked about his skills, but none were quite like this 2018 promotion vintage.

For Warnock to call his City success his "best by a mile" says it all about the astonishing turnaround he managed in his short time at the club.

"If you knew what I've had to do off the field as well as on the field," Warnock told the media in his final press conference, as ever able to get away with things others would feel the full force of their employers over. "I think it's an incredible feat. I said to the lads on Thursday, if things don't go right and we go into the playoffs, we've still had a great season. They're proud of being Bluebirds again, the fans. Everyone wants to support the club now and that's lovely. I know we're not easy on the eye. If I was paying money, as a Sheffield lad, my team were super. You knew you'd get criticised at times in certain games, but you can only work with what you've got, and I'm really proud to have built a team capable of ruffling a few feathers when I look at the teams below us in the division, with their budgets."

Warnock at his pragmatic best. Even in admitting this promotion wasn't the most pleasing, in purist terms, to watch, he still manages to give everyone at the club – players and, most of all fans – what they've been waiting for. It had felt a long time, too long, but they definitely were proud to be Bluebirds again. The fact that so many were out cheering the week after the Reading game showed that. For Dylan Pugh all that mattered was that City were up.

Others might not have such total emotional investment in the Bluebirds, but they do get near enough. That was plain to see in the thousands of like-minded people who'd shared in the elation that hot Sunday afternoon. That achievement meant so much to them.

Because of all that, because of where the club was and where it is now, the promotion will provide an emotional legacy for future generations of fans that past accomplishments simply could not. Put in those terms it's arguably as important as the 1993 Third Division title win and the FA Cup final of 2008.

Pride in the badge, in the colour and in the club had been rediscovered and restored. Cardiff City were up. They were up wearing blue. They played their football with courage, and they were led by someone who understood what it means to be a Bluebird better than anyone since the great Eddie May.

2

We'll Always Be Blue

"I'm not looking for excuses, just looking at myself and what I could have done better. I said no to Aston Villa because I was not ready. I said yes to Cardiff because I felt ready. But I was not."
Ole Gunnar Solskjær

Being a football fan is about much more than cheering your side's triumphs. Outside of the very top clubs it has to be. Success comes rarely to the rest of us. Of course it's about hope, but there is so much else that makes someone fall in love with their club. It's about smells and sounds and songs. About bonds. About a sense of place. It's about collective experiences and personal memories. It's tribal, raw and instinctive; inexplicable and baffling to outsiders, and yes, it's also very much about your team's colour.

It's in this primeval mix of emotions that comes an explanation for the utter euphoria in Cardiff City's promotion after the enmity of the years before. Because, to understand how and why Cardiff City got promoted in 2018, you need to look long before Neil Warnock's tenure, before even that of his predecessor, to the last time the club had a go, and failed so miserably, at Premier League football.

City could not have been a success under Warnock without having endured the mistakes, and their consequences, of a time long before he came along. Warnock was probably the only manager who could come into a club in the situation Cardiff City was, both because of his pure gutsiness as well as his footballing *nous*, and do what he did.

The profligate spending of two of Warnock's predecessors in many ways provided the spine for the squad which won promotion. The parts were there, though it may not have been obvious to us, and it simply needed Warnock to make them all tick.

After 51 years outside the top flight, the club had finally made it back in 2013. It was, in truth (though that was hardly admitted at the time), a club divided. Even for many fans who'd stuck by the team despite the change in colours from royal blue to red, it was a moment of bitter sweetness, and beating the Premier League champions Manchester City 3-2 at home in August remained the only real high point in a turgid season.

This was the rarest of chances for the club to stake a long-held claim by fans that it was one of the biggest in the land – and it ended more disastrously than anyone could have predicted. Malky Mackay, the man who had led the club to promotion, was sacked by December, his big spending summer badly judged – the spectre of £8m flop Andreas Cornelius, making up the numbers in reserve games totemic of City's calamitous first crack at the Premier League.

Mackay had already paid out an unprecedented amount to secure the club's promotion the season before, and City were among the biggest spenders in that summer transfer window, but they were hardly signings to build foundations for a future in the top division. The big names – Chile international Gary Medel and former Tottenham defender Steven Caulker – largely failed and it was left to players like Aron Gunnarsson, David

Marshall, Ben Turner and Kevin McNaughton (you might call them old-fashioned pros at the core of that squad) to fight to save some dignity from the calamitous adventure in the Premier League. Little dignity was salvaged.

As the season wore on and with things going wrong on the pitch, it was inevitable that the issue of the club colours would be a growing source of disquiet for everyone who followed City. Many accepted change if it meant securing the future of the club and bringing the kind of success they'd previously only dreamt of. Others had turned away from it, given up on the Bluebirds, and now had added reason to criticise.

What had been the point of it all in the first place? Red v Blue. Even more a source for anger, antipathy and antagonism than it had ever been before. Against the backdrop of protests and boycotts was an unfolding and unstoppable mess on the pitch.

In early January, Ole Gunnar Solskjær was appointed Mackay's successor after the Scot was sacked at the end of December. Solskjær had flown to Wales from Norway, where he was managing Molde, for talks with City chairman Mehmet Dalman – who said he felt like he was "the cat who got the cream" after he'd persuaded the former Manchester United striker to take the post. He was "100% convinced" the Norwegian was the right man.

Solskjær began with a win, against Newcastle in the FA Cup, before four defeats in a row. A 2-1 win against relegation rivals Norwich City was followed by an embarrassing 3-0 rout by Swansea City at the Liberty Stadium. That January transfer window saw another high turnover of players and some bewildering signings by Solskjær. His sights were set on his native Norway for players to help the Bluebirds break out of the relegation mire.

He lavished money on unknowns including, Magnus Wolff Eikrem, Mats Møller Dæhli and Jo Inge Berget. Big name striker Kenwyne Jones was added to the squad from Stoke City, while Solskjær returned to United to bring in full-back Fabio and winger Wilfried Zaha. Spanish defender Juan Cala was a forgettable deadline day signing.

Solskjær also attempted to change the style of play, from Mackay's high-tempo, aggressive football to the fast-paced pass-and-move stuff which had brought success for his old boss Sir Alex Ferguson at Manchester United. It was all too much too soon.

The second half of City's season in the Premier League was marked by disjointed performances with a defence full of leaks. Solskjær's naive tactics for a team at the bottom of the table, along with his strange team selections, compounded a sense of disillusionment among fans. Nobody could buy into what he was trying to achieve because nobody knew what that was. A nice guy, but a terrible fit as Cardiff City manager.

It was a struggle to watch, and the atmosphere at the Cardiff City Stadium was as dull come May 2014 as it had been loud the previous August. Four years later, the club would still be recovering.

Speaking to Norwegian broadcaster TV2 in 2016, Solskjær himself admitted: "I was not ready for it. I did not do a good job. I had three years of success with Molde, winning the League twice and the Cup. I thought I was fully prepared, that I was ready for the Premier League, but it's a completely different world there. Everything is much bigger. Norway is a small environment. There are only three to four agents to deal with, just 15 other clubs and that's it! I obviously was not ready for the entire Premier League showcase at a brand new club that I was not familiar with."

He also downplayed any external factors – the very public rift between his owner and predecessor and the fans' vociferous resentment over the club's colours – which might have helped him fail at Cardiff: "I'm not looking for excuses, just looking at myself and what I could have done better," he said. "I said no to Aston Villa because I was not ready. I said yes to Cardiff because I felt ready. But I was not."

That was all too evident in another muddled summer transfer window, where owner Vincent Tan consented to more of Solskjær's free-spending. Big money went out again, this time on Reading's prolific striker Adam le Fondre, the unknown Austrian forward Guido Burgstaller, the inexperienced midfielder Tom Adeyemi, the centre-half Sean Morrison – another from Reading – and the languid, but skilful defender Bruno Manga from French side Lorient.

Of Solskjær's signings it is only the latter two who've made a success of their time at City. The others, along with the hotchpotch of free transfers from around England and Europe, mainly failed to make it as Bluebirds. To the dismay of fans, captain Mark Hudson, having been talked of as the key man in the team and the leader in the dressing room that he needed, was allowed to leave for Huddersfield Town.

Moulding a team from all this and fostering any sort of harmony in the dressing room would have been difficult for the most seasoned of managers. For Solskjær, it was a job too big. He looked an increasingly dejected and powerless figure on the touchline as the new season began and results flip flopped from mediocre to dreadful. Selection seemed like a lottery at times, Le Fondre was confusingly played on the wing and there was a reluctance to stick to anything like a settled side. There were few reasons for fans to cheer as performances became even more directionless. City would not be making any quick return to the top flight under Solskjær, that much was becoming very obvious very quickly.

Five wins in 25 games was not a good enough record, and his exit was sealed after two consecutive home defeats in

September. It was an amicable separation, showing the then 41-year-old to be a likeable character, who Tan said would "always be welcome in the chairman's suite" as long as he was owner of the club. "During my short association with Ole, I have found him to be an honest and hardworking professional, but unfortunately the football results were not in his favour," Tan said.

Not only that, but Solskjær's transfer policy had left the club with a bloated squad, it had too many players and was patchy in quality.

Writing for *WalesOnline* on the eve of Solskjær's sacking, journalist Paul Abbandonato, who had been covering the fortunes of the club for more than two decades wrote: "Cardiff, under Solskjaer, [appeared] confused, chaotic, and clueless. They are like that because of his non-stop tinkering, which has led to a lack of consistency and pattern, and some truly crass decision-making when it comes to team selection." It was an experiment gone horribly wrong.

After his sacking, City legends Daniel Gabbidon and Scott Young were given responsibility for the first team while Tan set his sights on a successor for Solskjær. He identified his man, with the help – so we were told – of ex-West Ham manager Glenn Roeder, in Russell Slade.

With his match-day uniform, a training ground tracksuit and baseball cap, he was a contrast, physically, to the broad-shouldered Malky Mackay and svelte, still athletic Ole Gunnar Solskjær. Slade looked like a PE teacher. A hangover from when he taught at Frank Wheldon Comprehensive School in Nottingham. BT Sport commentator and former pupil Darren Fletcher told *WalesOnline* he used to get misbehaving pupils to box each other.

After the excesses and failures of his previous two appointments, Tan needed someone he could trust, and the unassuming Slade promised a less flashy approach. One thing was certain, Slade would not get anywhere near the amounts of cash that Solskjær and Mackay had put away on transfers in their time. Between them, the pair had spent nearly £60m of Tan's money in the preceeding three years.

In contrast, Slade's first January transfer signing in 2015 was the full-back Scott Malone – for £90,000. The £175,000 signing of striker Alex Revell from Rotherham later that month confirmed this new frugality at Cardiff City. In the summer window, Slade was given no money to spend, having to make do with a couple of free transfer signings and some loanees as the season went on.

Unheard-of Idriss Saadi, Jordan Blaise and the popular, if limited, Dutch playmaker Lex Immers, were hardly likely to light up the division, and they didn't. Put in that context Slade's job was remarkable. He kept the club in the division despite having some of the finest talent there being sold from under his feet. In his full season in charge, 2015-16, he got City to eighth in the league and in with a very real chance of a place in the play-offs almost until the end of the season. Despite all that, Slade remains one of the most unpopular Cardiff managers in living memory.

Danny Gabbidon gave some insight into the scale of the challenge Slade faced coming into the club.

Gabbidon had been re-signed in 2015 and before long found himself taking joint charge of the first team with Young after Solskjær left. Speaking to Blakey's Bootroom on *WalesOnline*, he revealed the schisms that dominated the dissonant dressing room which Slade had to manage: "Russell had a tough job when he came in, I know because I was there, there was a lot of stuff going on," said Gabbidon. "There were players who needed to be shifted, bad eggs. The squad was very large, there were two groups. There was a lot to sort out before he even thought about how the team played. He's straightforward in how he wants the team to play, it was about getting the right people in the right positions and getting them to gel and I don't think that was happening at the start."

Slade's critics – and there were many – pointed out that he was still managing a squad of players assembled by his predecessors who'd forked out millions to bring them to Cardiff. One acquisition of note, however, a few months after joining the Bluebirds, was when he brought in Paul Trollope, the highly-rated coach who, during his time with the club, would go on to be a part of Chris Coleman's successful management team with Wales. It was a shrewd move. Trollope added – for a few games at least – some energy and spark into the sluggish performances which had become the standard under Slade.

Trollope's body language on the touchline, forceful and animated, gave the impression that he was adding some tactical knowledge which had been lacking. It was a contrast to Slade – always standing, arms folded, at the edge of his technical area – critics suggesting how little he was interested in directing things on the pitch.

With Wales' success under Coleman too, Trollope's arrival gave supporters a sense that the club understood them and what they wanted to see happening at the Cardiff City Stadium because, at that time, the Bluebirds were drifting and directionless. Crowds were ebbing away after the relegation and as the emotive issue of the club's colours grew ever more contentious. The atmosphere at the ground felt increasingly drab, goals felt rare, few fans even bothered to jeer instead of cheer as mediocrity set in.

The momentum built from the new stadium and the Wembley appearances was slowing to a stop.

Perceptions matter in football, and supporters began to turn away from the club as it entered a period of austerity and the owner sought a new, more measured approach to its transfer policy. By 2015-16, Slade's one full season in charge, the average home attendance had withered to 16,000. When the club moved into the new ground, that average figure stood around 20,000 – reaching the 27,000 mark when they were playing in the Premier League.

The one thing which had become as familiar as vacant seats in the half-empty stadium was the sound of the back-to-blue anthem, sung on the stroke of 27 minutes – that most important of numbers for Cardiff City fans – at every match: "We'll always be blue, we'll always be blue – we're Cardiff City, we'll always be blue!" Followed, every time, by rousing chants of "BLUEBIRDS! BLUEBIRDS! BLUEBIRDS!" It was a sign of some growing unity on the terraces, and a shifting culture at the club.

The final game of City's Premier League season, against Chelsea, marked just how much the mood among fans had changed. Abbandonato wrote: "The *We'll Always Be Blue* chant was sung with more force and gusto that Sunday afternoon than at any other point. There was no turning back from here."

As late as December 2014, Tan was adamant that the team would continue to play in red, but the colour issue had become toxic. By the middle of the first season back in the Championship it was dominating everything, and with performances so weak on the pitch, fans vented their anger at the direction the club was taking – with the now almost universally reviled rebrand at the centre of their fury.

Things came to a head in a meeting at the start of 2015 – organised at the request of an obviously concerned Tan – held between Mehmet Dalman, chief executive Ken Choo and City supporters.

It was clear that the deep discord inside the club was now a very real worry to its hierarchy.

Tan was hated. The red affair had dragged on for two years, during which time protest group Bluebirds Unite had collected signatures on a petition, begging for him to reconsider the rebrand, and the Irish *Mirror* published "10 ways to p*** off Vincent Tan – a comprehensive guide for Cardiff City Fans."

Within 24 hours of the meeting, Tan gave supporters an overdue Christmas present, and an unlikely mascot: "The Christmas and New Year period has given me time to reflect on the events of the last year," he said. After all the posturing, the threats to leave and the cocky defiance, Tan finally relented and announced he'd had a change of heart.

Apparently, thousands of angry fans and a ridiculing media don't scare him – but – like most of us – he couldn't handle being on the wrong side of his mum. "Spending time with my family," he continued, "had a profound effect upon me. My mother, Madam Low Siew Beng, a devout Buddhist, who attended Cardiff City Football Club to watch them play, spoke to me on the importance of togetherness, unity and happiness. Cardiff City Football Club is important to me and I wish to see it united and happy."

Tan promised City would play in blue from that moment on – after being granted special permission from the Football League to do so mid-season – as well as a redesign of the club's badge the next season which would reinstate the prominence of the Bluebird on the crest. With the attendance issue now a concern, the back-to-blue announcement was packaged up with a price-freeze on season ticket prices.

The development was supposed to add an injection of passion into the season, and it did for a little while, but the wounds inflicted by the divisions at Cardiff City would take much longer to heal than a few days. Promotion success had masked the discomfort felt so deeply by so many at watching the club they love play in a colour so alien to their traditions.

Pragmatists had argued it didn't matter. The fact City had won a promotion to the Premier League, with attendances actually boosted in this brave new scarlet era, was proof. Success, for most fans and their clubs, is rare and fleeting, however. So when City fell out of the top league as quickly as they had arrived, it was almost inevitable that the colour of the kit would matter much more than when millions of pounds were being pumped into transfers.

A carnival atmosphere was promised for the first game back in blue – a 1-0 win over Fulham at home on January 10, 2015, but the party was almost over before it had begun. A winter storm had ravaged the British Isles, causing massive travel disruption, bringing down trees and damaging buildings. The gales had also struck a blow at the stadium, tearing off cladding, prompting safety concerns and doubts that the game would be played at all. Just like the club's faltering relationship with fans, the stadium was patched up.

Ken Choo and Mehmet Dalman went on a lap of honour around the pitch before the match, shaking hands, signing autographs, performing the obligatory 'ayatollah' salute. Fans proudly held their blue scarves above their heads and *We'll Always Be Blue* was sung with even more oomph. The foundation stones of a new era of bridge-building had been put in place. Things began to feel more positive.

Slade said he hoped the move would spark some momentum on the pitch and give the team a chance to power up the division and into the play-offs. Ultimately, though, much more was needed than a statement of regret, a switch back to royal blue and a pitchside walk by City's senior officials, to truly unite supporters and provide a sense of togetherness that meant something.

Many fans had by now fallen out of the habit of going to the football. It doesn't take long for families to find new Saturday afternoon pursuits. There are many more attractive options than going to a lifeless Cardiff City Stadium and watching 90 minutes of anaemic football on a cold, wet day in the middle of winter.

What did this mean? Despite the return to blue and competitive season ticket pricing, the self-inflicted era of austerity and unimaginative style of play under Slade kept away supporters who'd already found alternative weekend interests and stopped others from bothering to return. Slade's one full season in charge was a disappointment.

There were glimmers, like the 2-0 win over rivals Bristol City at Ashton Gate, where Slade signings Stuart O'Keefe and Lex Immers both scored. It was a win which gave impetus to the faint hopes of promotion, but as winter turned to spring, these hopes shrivelled and City's mediocrity pushed them out of contention for a play-off place.

Losing 3-0 at Sheffield Wednesday in the Bluebirds' final away game of the season was pathetic. The 1-1 draw against Birmingham City in the last match of the season at the Cardiff City Stadium proved a fittingly uninspirational end to the Slade era.

Before that match was played, the club had announced Slade would not be manager the next season, instead he was to be moved upstairs in a role as head of football. Fans, who'd seen the success of Swansea City down the M4, where the club had developed its own brand of football and playing style – the self-declared Swansea Way – had felt such an appointment was needed at Cardiff.

Slade was now in place to bridge the gap between owner and manager, via the club chairman and chief executive and help create that new football identity. He fitted that role, if nothing else he was an experienced football man, trusted by the board.

"It was nice at the end," an emotional Slade said after the Birmingham game. He'd just been given a standing ovation by the few fans who'd waited for the traditional end-of-season walkabout by players and staff. "It was nice to have that rapport and that relationship which has grown with the fans over my time here. It's not quite enough, we know that, but at least we have stability. When I came to the club, we were 17th. We managed to stop that slide, turn it around, address the financial side, reduce the wage bill."

That was it. Slade's tenure was over. The end of his role at Cardiff City as unremarkable as many of his matches. He will be remembered for the boring football, the lack of possession, the infrequent attacking play and the rare goals. In raw emotional terms, Slade was a failure – but he was also one of the best things to happen to City. Why? He was what the club needed after the whirlwind years of Mackay and Solskjær.

Throughout that full season of Slade football, fans may have hated his team's lack of adventure, but there was no budging the club. That's probably because, in reality, he did exactly the job he had to do. He rescued Cardiff from the prospect of relegation, he managed to get his team to eighth in the division the next season, and he did that as the club cut costs and frantically tried to make good the extravagance of recent years.

A couple of weeks after being appointed head of football, Slade left City in search of a new managerial job (the new 'off the training field' role perhaps not one for him) and he was already heavily linked with the vacancy at Charlton Athletic, where he was later appointed.

What next? For Cardiff City, 2016 was to be a summer of rebuilding. The club needed the Slade era to take a deep breath from all the drama that had preceded him. Fans had watched jaw-dropping spends, they celebrated a promotion and wept at a relegation, they'd protested and complained and won the battle to bring back blue (with a bit of help from Tan's mum). They'd also endured the consequences of all that intense emotion – in the nondescript football of those Slade 18 months which followed. There had been a transfer embargo – it was found the club had flouted Football League financial fair play rules. Attendances were dripping away.

The future was uncertain.

Supporters were taking refuge from the pessimism at Leckwith in the success of the Wales team on the brink of doing something special in France at the European Championships. A familiarly gloomy mood pervaded for Bluebirds fans, used to disappointment but itching to feel some enthusiasm and passion from the club. They needed a lift. They craved optimism as the club searched for a new manager, hoping a new appointment would get them excited about their team again after so many false starts.

The same old names were linked, but there were some interesting ones, too. Could something different be about to happen? Could a young, hungry, talented coach take this Cardiff City side – still filled with quality players – to new glories?

3

Europe and All That

"When I took the job I knew what it entailed, I knew where we
were as a club and what I thought we needed to move forward."

Paul Trollope

European adventures and misadventures – the summer of
2016 was one dominated by continental questions. How would
Wales do in the European Championship finals in France?
Which way would the UK vote in the EU referendum?

Future generations of A-level history students will study the
origins, causes and effects of the Brexit vote – and its polarising
consequences mirrored how the blue/red issue had split Cardiff
City friendships and divided families. Cardiff fans were well
prepared for debates on intractable issues with unwavering
opinions.

Football provided relief from the interminable democratic
chaos and squabbling – and it was thanks to Europe. Chris
Coleman's brilliant Wales side had been the succour for City
supporters bored, annoyed or demoralised by the subject of
colour. While some voters at home trooped to the polling
stations to vote in favour of Brexit, thousands of Wales fans in

France were counting on the national team and enjoying even greater European integration as the finals went on.

It was a sign of how much the Wales team had developed during the tournament that losing to eventual winners, Portugal, was a real disappointment. What if former Cardiff City midfielder Aaron Ramsey had not been suspended for that semi-final in Lyon? It proved a step too far for Wales, especially without the Arsenal midfielder and Ben Davies, the Spurs defender, as second-half goals from Ronaldo and Nani saw the nation's hopes, in our first major finals since 1958, crushed.

Perhaps more than anything – more, even, than proof that a nation of three million can compete with the best in the world – Wales' French adventure proved how massive and unifying football can be for the country. The travelling thousands, dubbed the Red Wall by the players, provided the most memorable, lyrical and loudest atmospheres witnessed at any of the tournament's fixtures. Their gleeful yet peaceful conduct was a stark contrast to the troubled history of England's football support overseas.

The Eiffel Tower had been lit in red, white and green after the win over Slovakia and *L'Equipe*, the French sports daily, reported glowingly of the impact Wales fans were having. The rendition of the national anthem was 'a hymn to give you goosebumps', wrote Vincent Garcia. The newspaper described Wales as a 'new sensation', and its supporters' 'tolerance of drink' was a welcome attribute to the French hosts as England and Russia fans clashed violently in Marseilles. It exemplified the cheerful patriotic goodwill which had become the hallmark of following Wales since the appointment of Gary Speed as manager: the best behaved, best voiced fans – if only Cardiff City could capture some of that magic.

Ordinarily, such a success for Wales would not impact much on the fortunes or direction of Cardiff City. This time, however, the national team's success was important for the Bluebirds. The club's leadership was watching with great interest as Wales showed they were one of the best teams in world football with a top ten FIFA ranking. The managerial seat was vacant and a coach heralded as one of the key components in Coleman's managerial staff was already employed at the club – Paul Trollope.

Trollope's reputation was growing, and he was spoken of as one of the British game's most highly rated coaches. Coleman had appointed him to his cadre after Kit Symons departed to take charge of Fulham in the summer of 2015.

Cardiff City did not stand in the way, instead (and with a view to the future coaching structure at the club) encouraged Trollope – who won nine caps for his country – to become involved with the national side. He would be working alongside Coleman and the respected FAW technical director Osian Roberts as well as with players like Ramsey, Gareth Bale, Joe Allen and Ashley Williams. It would mean him bringing new ideas on training and tactics back to the club; plotting the defeats of teams like Belgium and Russia could only benefit players when Trollope returned from international duty to Cardiff's Vale of Glamorgan training ground.

By summer 2016, a belief was also beginning to pervade the club's hierarchy that, after the recent rollercoaster years – on and off the pitch – there was a need to replicate the success of rivals Swansea City and their so-called Swansea Way. City were after someone to devise a Cardiff Way, to draw up a blueprint for long-term success by utilising and bringing through local talent via the academy, and to develop a single playing style that would be embraced and perfected from the juniors to the senior squad.

Maybe this seemed ambitious, but another approach to finding winning football was needed after the careless spending and short-termism that had landed the club in such a difficult position. It appeared Trollope was just the man to do that. His record as a manager was mixed – if a little underwhelming – with his only real experience of being in charge coming at Bristol Rovers.

Appointed as Rovers' caretaker-manager in 2005, while still a player, Trollope impressed the club's board and was soon given the role of head coach, assisted by former City boss Lennie Lawrence who had been brought in as director of football to guide the young coach's development. During the pair's five-year reign at Rovers, Trollope took the team to the FA Trophy final in 2007 and led the side to promotion – via the play-offs – to League One. He also led Rovers to the quarter-finals of the FA Cup in 2008, when their impressive run was ended by Premier League side Fulham.

When Lawrence left Rovers in May 2010, the director of football role wasn't filled and Trollope was appointed manager, with complete control of the Bristol club, but was sacked halfway through the season with the team struggling in the League One relegation zone. However, despite his problems managing Rovers, Trollope's coaching talent remained, and soon after leaving the County Ground he was taken on as coach by Chris Hughton at Norwich City.

Trollope's was not the only name linked with the vacant manager's job at Cardiff City, as 17 other candidates were apparently interviewed by the club – with former England boss Steve McLaren among those interested. City coach James Rowberry was also touted as a favourite, but on May 18 it was Trollope who was named the new Bluebirds manager – official title: head coach – tasked with drawing a line under past regimes and bringing a new style and concept of football philosophy.

You could see what City were after from Trollope in the statements made following his appointment. Vincent Tan said he expected him to implement an "attractive style of football that Cardiff City fans love". Tan described him as "young, full of ideas, extremely hard working" and "we hope that under Paul's leadership, Cardiff City will return to the Premier League. I'd like to thank him for what he's done for us so far whilst wishing him the best of luck for the future." The pressure was already on the 44-year-old.

Trollope himself knew his job was to turn City into a new footballing force without squandering any of the club's money. His age, his place as a respected coach, and his playing background as a grafting pro who made it to a Wales international despite his limitations as a midfielder, were all elements which made him a handsome choice for the Bluebirds.

He would still be travelling to France with Wales that summer, and would rejoin City for pre-season training once the tournament was over. There was also an appeal in building something identifiably Welsh at the club too. If Sam Hammam had tried, unsuccessfully, to do something similar more than a decade earlier, then Trollope promised a more intelligent and thoughtful go at creating a Cardiff City Way, and two of his signings that summer would confirm his approach to the role.

Trollope admitted that "promotion has got to be the aim".

"We have to be ambitious," he said on the day he was unveiled.

"We have to create a positivity and a real belief within the club. Not just down the training ground, the staff and the players, but we need that real belief throughout the club. If we can do that and taking that step – and it is a big step – with that unity and wise recruitment, that's what we will be looking to take.

"If we make a good start and we're in the mix then promotion has got to be the aim."

Though there was a sense that Trollope would be given time – and that supporters of course wanted him to be a success – the response of City fans was an anti-climax.

'Not inspiring and doesn't fill me with promise but I wish him well and success. We all want that I'm sure,' tweeted Nigel Harris (@NigelBlues), replying to the club's announcement on Twitter.

Others were less diplomatic. Damian Hern (@damo563) wrote: 'wow and the verdict so far is an underwhelming appointment...but you can't please everybody...but pleasing nobody...#epicfail'.

Another said Trollope was an "underwhelming" choice. Elliott Canter commented: 'No ambition, same old cheap choices. When will we learn?'

There were also worries amongst fans that Trollope's absence while away on Wales duty would be a problem for City, but that wasn't an issue for the club, which wanted Trollope to gain as much as possible from the Euros.

Whatever else, this was a new start. The new head coach reunited himself with former City boss Lennie Lawrence, while performance specialist Ryland Morgans, who worked with Trollope at Wales, was also recruited as part of his coaching team to improve fitness.

It was yet another summer of change, the end at City for numerous players signed when times were good and money was flowing more freely from the owner's bank account. The brakes on the spending were really on.

Out went Fabio, Eoin Doyle, Scott Malone, Kagisho Dikgacoi, Kenwyne Jones and Filip Kiss. Of those, City fans were only sad, perhaps, to see Fabio depart. The Brazilian full-back had become a crowd favourite for his commitment, as well as the guile he showed in every game. That summer was also the end for Ben Turner, the centre-half who had shone in the first half of City's season in the Premier League – enjoying the kind of consistency which had seen him become one of the best defenders in the Championship – but who had become increasingly injury prone.

Gone also, and to the sadness of so many Bluebirds supporters, was David Marshall, arguably the finest goalkeeper in the Championship. Marshall's form in the Premier League for Cardiff had resulted in the club losing many games by much finer margins than they truly deserved, and he probably ensured relegation was avoided until April.

Along with Bruno Manga, he was the most consistent player for Russell Slade, and the decision to sell Marshall to Hull City – who had just won promotion under Steve Bruce – was arguably made with his welfare in mind (that's not to ignore the £2m profit the club made on the Scotland international). He deserved another crack at the top flight and he would not be getting it with City that year, and probably not the season after, either.

Trollope's signings also gave a hint about what he and the club wanted to establish. He brought in Jazz Richards from Fulham in a swap deal with Malone. The former Swansea full-back, pacey and adventurous (and prone to the odd mistake), was a part of Coleman's Wales revolution and the sort of player who would thrive in this new Cardiff City environment.

In too came Emyr Huws, a talented young player who'd never quite made the grade at the top level. Wales fans had seen him as a midfielder with plenty of skill and ability – an eye for a pass and a gift for scoring brilliant goals – and it was hoped a team could be built around him, or at least he could be part of something exciting, young and energetic. Huws had been playing for Wigan Athletic in League One and jumped at the chance to join City in the Championship.

If those two signings excited, the others barely raised fans' pulses. Kenneth Zohore, a striker signed on loan during the club's financial fair play transfer embargo the previous season, became a permanent deal, with no-one foreseeing the player he would become. Freddie Gounongbe was brought in from Belgian team Westerlo on a free transfer, popular midfielder Lex Immers became a permanent signing, while talented left-back Joe Bennett was also deftly added to the squad.

On deadline day, with the Bluebirds in desperate need of a proven striker, Trollope turned to his old Bristol Rovers centre forward Rickie Lambert, who'd since forged a serious career (despite his age) in the Premier League – at first with Southampton and then with Liverpool. The Scouser had been capped by England despite having spent the first half of his career bouncing around lower league football clubs before heading to the south coast to help Southampton's return to the Premier League. His transfer fee – around £1.7m – and age – 34 when he signed for the club – left question marks over the signing, but Trollope was confident he'd be a success. This was a player with international pedigree who'd been prolific at almost all of his previous clubs and he was exactly the type of forward City were in need of.

While Trollope wheeled and dealed on the transfer market, pre-season preparations were not going exactly to plan for City. Fittingly, in light of the new European model at the club (and Cardiff's 60%-40% vote to remain in the EU) the Bluebirds had scheduled a pre-season tour to Germany, which included a hastily rearranged match with RW Ahlen due to an unplayable pitch.

On arrival at the Weserstadion, City staff had found the pitch was just an appalling patchwork of divots and far from fit to host a competitive pre-season friendly. Both teams then rushed over to City's training camp ground and kicked off at 8pm local time, before abandoning the match altogether, with thunderstorms posing a risk to players and a lack of floodlights at the site meaning darkness would end any chance of continuing for a full 90 minutes anyway.

Trollope spoke of his frustration at the calamity, stating that his players had been prepared and readied for the clash. A small tournament held at Osnabrück saw City beat both the hosts and St Pauli, with Gounongbe among the pick of the Bluebirds players. The final pre-season match before City kicked off their campaign against Birmingham saw the club travel to the English south coast to play Bournemouth, with the Bluebirds hoping to find their own version of young, bright manager Eddie Howe in Trollope.

They lost 1-0 to the Premier League side but it was no embarrassment, although City's lack of goals, which continued into the start of the season, was a worry despite Lambert's arrival.

The Trollope revolution was fully underway by now and the new manager positioned himself as one of football's deep thinkers. City would have more flexible tactics, deploying the wing-back system that had brought success for Wales. With energetic and attack-minded full-backs – Joe Bennett, Declan John and Jazz Richards – Trollope had the players he needed for his preferred formation.

"We have focused on ourselves in pre-season and that will be the same during the season," Trollope said speaking before the season was underway. "If we get our physical shape, our tactical work and detail right we feel we can be confident because we have quality. We have players who have played in the Premier League and that is where we want to get back to."

The pressure for Trollope to hit the ground running that season with a string of victories was not just coming from the very top of the club, it was coming from Trollope – and he was backing himself to do that. He knew Tan expected a return to the Premier League, despite the players who'd gone – after all he was still being allowed to spend a decent amount of money on a number of players.

Results that August, however, would give a taste of the dismal standards in the brief Trollope era. A 0-0 draw against Birmingham was followed by a 2-0 home loss to QPR, which drew boos from the City Stadium crowd and further doubts from cynical supporters about the quality of the board's managerial appointment. Two games in and there were already questions being asked about the usefulness of his tactics in the Championship. Where was the club heading after the post-Premier League fall-out of the last two seasons? Where was the ambition? Where was the will to succeed? Was the club really serious about mounting a promotion campaign?

City lacked punch in attack (the signing of Lambert before the transfer window closed didn't really address this problem) and the tactics used by Trollope were criticised for their naivety. Fans took to messageboards and social media to vent their criticism: a poor system, the wrong players, a lack of quality and pace in key areas. Trollope's team, in their eyes, wasn't going to make much of an impact on the division – and even before August was over there were some who thought the Bluebirds looked more like relegation candidates than promotion-seeking high-flyers.

Victory did, at last, come in a win over Blackburn Rovers, although both Cardiff's goals in the 2-1 victory were scored by Rovers centre-half Shane Duffy (who'd be signed by Brighton before the transfer window closed). It was joked that goal-shy City's top scorer didn't even play for the club.

This was a time when City fans needed humour, the football was as underwhelming as it had been the previous season under Russell Slade. City picked up another point that August at Fulham, before a four-match losing streak piled the pressure on the beleaguered Trollope. The losing run started with a defeat by Reading at home, in which City looked toothless and lacking in spirit, then away losses at Norwich and Preston (with City's defence leaking six goals in those games) came before the Bluebirds lost at home to ex-Swansea manager Garry Monk's Leeds United – consigning the club to the bottom of the league. It had to be Leeds, and it had to be Garry Monk.

Rather than the new Cardiff City Way, which was supposed to bring a new sense of optimism to the club, the start of the season had turned into a disaster. In the face of such disillusionment, the City head coach remained upbeat and maintained that his side were continuing to create chances. He also spoke of the continued support he was being given by Tan, chairman Mehmet Dalman and chief executive Ken Choo.

Speaking to BBC Wales after the Leeds loss, Trollope said: "I thought we were in pretty good control, we needed one of the chances to go in and they didn't. The refereeing decision changed the game, which was frustrating for us because there was a lot going on at set-pieces at both ends. I'm not saying it wasn't a penalty but if he's giving it then he could be giving a few at either end."

Fans didn't hold back on social media following the Leeds defeat. 'Absolutely shocking performance,' wrote Michael Baldwin (@mickeyccfc1990). 'Wrong team selection from the start. Trollope is out of his depth just like [Slade] was.' Another (@Yerlydave) said: 'No creativity, no effort going forward. Get a manager that knows what he's doing. It's really hard to watch. Embarrassing.'

By now, there were the dozens of tweets calling for #TrollopeOut.

It was early days in the season for such a backlash, relegation is never settled in September, but there was a perception, among a large chunk of City's following who did not buy into the new philosophy, that Trollope was out of his depth before a game had even kicked off.

As September wore on, City managed to win away at Rotherham, before two defeats on the trot – at home to Derby and away to Burton – spelled the end for Trollope's stint in charge.

Not only were results causing very real worries about City's chances of staying in the Championship, they were also continuing to affect attendances. In this, the third season out of the Premier League, the reality was that fewer people wanted to watch a struggling side fail to produce wins or goals. Public relations had been improved with the return to blue, but that had not come with the desire the Cardiff crowd want to see from their Bluebirds team. Everything was so ordinary. It was as though the squad had already accepted it was to be a season of struggle, relegation a *fait accompli*. Fans could not stand that prospect, and nor did Trollope want that.

Speaking before the Rotherham win, he told the media he loved being City boss and wanted to give fans the winning team he thought they deserved. "I'm very proud to be in this position," he said. "I love the job and enjoy working with the staff and players. I've received so much support, it's been fantastic, it really has. When I took the job I knew what it entailed, I knew where we were as a club and what I thought we needed to move forward."

He talked again of his frustration with the way things had gone for him and his team, and believed luck to have run against them more often than not. Cardiff City fans disagreed. A good barometer of where the club was and where it was heading was in the attendances for those first couple of months of the season.

A hardcore of 15,000 continued to stick with the side but crowds were reaching worrying new lows. The first home game against QPR had an attendance of 15,869 – hardly the numbers you'd expect for the home opener – and none of which had the atmosphere the stadium had been used to in its early years. Attendances were back down to Ninian Park levels. In a stadium with a capacity of 34,000, the place felt empty, soulless. Trollope's final home game against Derby fell below the 15,000 level. His time at the club was quickly drawing to a close.

Defeat at Burton was too much for Tan – and City fans, singing "Sacked in the morning, you're getting sacked in the morning," knew it. The press had already reported on two crisis meetings held between Trollope and the club, but he was given their backing to continue and ploughed on in charge until October.

With City firmly in the relegation places now, something had to be done to halt an unstoppable rot. At the most recent of those crisis meetings he'd been given the chance to turn things around in three matches but, after the loss to Burton, Tan and his leading executives had no choice but to sack Trollope.

On October 4 the club announced he was leaving his post. It was a moment which was to prove one of the most pivotal in recent history at Cardiff City. 'Cardiff City Football Club can confirm that Paul Trollope's contract has been terminated with immediate effect,' a club statement said. 'We'd like to thank Paul for his efforts and wish him the very best of luck for the future. Assistant coach Lennie Lawrence and performance director Ryland Morgans have also left the club with our best wishes. An announcement regarding Paul's successor will be made in due course.'

The results of the Trollope experiment had come quickly, and they were negative. In the end it was no real surprise, but there was sadness that Trollope – talked of as one of the 'good guys' in the game and with a continued reputation as a quality coach – hadn't been able to make the job a success. Fans had endured 11 games and seen their side win only twice. There were too many defeats and far too few goals scored.

Trollope's side lacked the bite demanded by Bluebirds supporters. There was too much passing across the back and not enough penetration into opposition boxes. Poet Sarah McCreadie, 26, has been a City fan all her life. Her view on the Trollope disaster? It's that thing called identity again. "If I had to think of the main reason Trollope failed, I would say it was because back then we were a team with no identity," she says. "We seemed ultimately aimless and directionless during that period – on and off the field."

The paucity of goals was infuriating – only eight had been scored by the time Trollope left, three months into the season. Of course, City's slide into the relegation zone (they were 23rd in the Championship at this point) was of most concern, players were obviously short of confidence and it hardly looked as though there was a chance that the dire run of results could be turned around under Trollope. Sometimes football clubs have to take drastic decisions on their managers – it's the only means they have of arresting their freefall.

Trollope had been appointed on the wave of optimism which came with Wales' European Championship finals qualification. Ultimately, Wales' success in that tournament almost certainly hindered Trollope in his job as Cardiff manager – by the time the national team had lost to Portugal in the semi-final, pre-season training was already weeks old.

The club had to make the break with Trollope to save the season. As soon as the announcement was made, there was one favourite for the post. Cardiff City were about to make an appointment which would change everything.

4

Red Adair

"I want fans to go home talking about the shots, the saves, the offsides and the manager going stupid on the sidelines. That's what I love about football."

Neil Warnock

2016 was the year we all got headline fatigue. A Brexit vote, Donald Trump in the White House, the deaths of David Bowie, Prince, George Michael, Carrie Fisher and Muhammad Ali. On October 5, 2016, those who'd turned off the news may not have noticed Cardiff City Football Club signing a man named Neil Warnock as the club's manager.

Outspoken, sweary, and ambitious – Neil Warnock had a reputation for half-time rants and falling out with supporters and managers. How would he get on with his infamous new boss, Tan? Was he too hot-headed to lead a team in crisis?

There's a famous moment in a documentary following his time at Sheffield United where he launches into his captain Chris Morgan in the dressing room after a torrid first-half. Then there was Warnock's spat with Liverpool's Phil Thompson, again back in his Blades days, where he raged at the then Reds coach: "You can fuck off Pinocchio, get back in your fucking cupboard."

Warnock's long-running feud with old rival Stan Ternent is the stuff of legend. He actually wrote in his autobiography that he 'wouldn't piss on' the ex-Burnley boss 'if he was on fire'. He's certainly not scared of controversy. Or telling others the truth as he sees it.

"Warnock came in and shook the whole place up," said Sarah McCreadie. "Nobody was scared to play us back then [under Trollope], but they were under Warnock."

If it's possible to start again at a football club with the season already underway, then Warnock somehow managed it at Cardiff. His first game in charge was a crucial derby match against Bristol City – broadcast live on Sky – just a few days after he came in.

Living up to his reputation for craftiness in the transfer market, Warnock had brought in the defender Sol Bamba and forward Junior Hoilett – both would go on to become two of the most important players in City's promotion year.

Cardiff was the sort of job Warnock has always savoured. Through his career, he'd gone into clubs in need of sorting out – he turned Notts County from relegation candidates in the old Third Division into a top flight side; he saved Torquay from going into the conference; he got struggling Huddersfield Town promoted; and the season before coming to Cardiff, he'd extraordinarily rescued Rotherham United's Championship status.

Warnock, in his first interview after he was unveiled, told City's official website that the "whole club needs a lift." He then added: "Rest assured I'll be providing entertainment. I want fans to go home talking about the shots, the saves, the offsides and the manager going stupid on the sidelines. That's what I love about football."

His sparkle was in contrast to his predecessor's anodyne soundbites, and journalists loved it. "You know he's going to give you gold, he's going to give you a line – whatever's been the talking point of that week, he's going to provide something," said Dom Booth, who covered City's promotion season for *WalesOnline*.

Honesty will get you everywhere and nowhere in football, maybe that's why Warnock is so well-travelled without ever having had a crack at a big Premier League club. "I've always liked it [at Cardiff]," he said on his arrival in Wales. "Everywhere I go I get stick but I've always had good banter with the Cardiff people. They're my type of crowd – blood and guts and all that, which I like – and I know that if I can get it right for them, they'll get behind me. I enjoy challenges and the challenge at the moment is to get the team higher up the league and then we'll see how we go."

What were Cardiff fans in for? They'd soon find out in that first match against Bristol City, which now had the Warnock factor (his history with the Ashton Gate club and manager Lee Johnson and Johnson's dad, Gary, would ensure that) to enliven it, as well as it being a derby. Johnson, whose spat with Warnock came the previous season – when Bristol played Rotherham – after the Yorkshireman had made pre-match comments hinting that his side would use "aggression, good football or intimidation" to win. In response, Johnson had described Warnock as a "pantomime villain". Pantomimes can be fine pieces of entertainment and the villain of the piece the most entertaining thing of all.

Sky must have been overjoyed they'd chosen to show this one. City won 2-1. A crowd of more than 22,746 was there, and Sol Bamba got on the scoresheet (he was immediately labelled a "cult hero").

The game lived up to expectations – played with an intensity and tempo which had been absent from City matches for years – the victory was a relief to fans who'd tolerated so many hours of drab football that season.

There must have been cheek-puffing sighs of relief in the boardroom, too. The Trollope appointment was a clear error but maybe they'd got it right with Warnock? His first run of matches in charge would quickly provide the answer. Four days after the win over Bristol City, Warnock took on his old hometown rivals, Sheffield Wednesday. It was a game with obvious personal meaning for the Sheffield United man.

Before kick-off, the 50th anniversary of the Aberfan disaster was marked with a moving minute's silence in memory of its 128 victims. It must have emphasised to Warnock the importance of the old coalfield communities to the club and its similarities to the industrial tradition of his native northern England. The match ended 1-1, a fair result in the end and a good point for City, with Wednesday dominating possession and looking as though they'd be play-off contenders at the very least by the end of the season.

The last of his first three games was away at Nottingham Forest, and this one too had resonance. Forest was a club with its own problems and one which Warnock has admitted he'd like to manage. In fact, and luckily for City, he'd been turned down for the Forest job a few months before. "I talked to a nice chap there throughout the summer and it just was not meant to be at that time," he told BBC Wales before the match. "I am a massive believer in fate. This fits me far better, my type of place, two-and-a-half hours from home as well. You don't get many opportunities like that."

He had led Notts County up through the divisions some 30 years previously, while never hiding his admiration for Forest's great manager Brian Clough. In his autobiography, Warnock admits he 'hero-worshipped' Clough. 'I knew I wasn't going to get a top club job,' he wrote. 'I knew I was always going to get struggling clubs that needed a Red Adair. That's why I liked what he did. He was the underdog a lot of the time but he showed that the underdog could still come out on top. That's why he was the best to me. I spent more time studying him and admiring him than anybody else.'

City won the match at the City Ground 2-1, with midfielders Aron Gunnarsson and Joe Roals scoring the goals. That was seven points from nine and City out of the relegation places. Football's Red Adair was enjoying his latest firefight.

Look at the possession stats from those three games and they don't bear much comparison to Russell Slade's time. Cardiff's opponents had most of the ball, but City had more shots and more shots on target. Most importantly, they had more points. The lack of possession under Warnock hardly matters when the team is flying, it's when things go wrong that it can look its most ugly – fans and football writers tend to forget about long balls if it means excitement around the penalty area.

So far, City fans hadn't seen much of that, because it had been a thrilling week for them – a new manager, new players, wins and a move up the table to ease concerns about relegation. Warnock was even questioned about the chances of promotion after that string of results: "We just get carried away, don't we?" came the terse reply.

Over the coming months, City slowly climbed away from the relegation places. There were blips along the way, but defeats were now increasingly isolated amid runs of draws and wins. It was the kind of form which would have got them into the play-offs, but the season ended just too soon – or at least Warnock had come into the club a month or two too late.

As important as promotion that season, was the continuing effort to reunite fans with the club. Cardiff could have appointed any other manager but nobody else could have affected the atmosphere at the Cardiff City Stadium quite like Warnock.

"Neil Warnock was perfect for Cardiff City," says Booth. The honour in underdog status, the desire to prove others wrong – all proud elements in Warnock's character are also traits in

Bluebirds' supporters. "I've got a few friends who are City fans and they love that he loves to upset people."

His charisma and leadership were uniting its still divided support.

The club had already done much to repair the damage done by the switch to red shirts, it was now having to also work to bring back lost fans, fed up with the football played by their team. Crowds struggled, even after Warnock arrived. There were spikes – among them the game against Aston Villa which City won 1-0 and the final match of the season versus promoted Newcastle United – but also plenty of dips which must have been a concern. A game against Preston in January 2017 was watched by just 13,894.

By the end of the season the average home gate at the Cardiff City Stadium was 16,564, well below the number when the club first moved across Sloper Road from Ninian Park in 2009. The healing process was taking time.

Many of those turned away by the colour change still hadn't come back, while the style and standard of football of the previous three seasons must also have been a factor in keeping attendances down.

Warnock wanted to change things. But how did he do it?

"He got everyone moving in the same direction," says author and City fan James Leighton, who points to Warnock's honesty and frankness as probably the most important of his character traits in winning back supporters. "I liked how he went out into the valleys and to clubs around south Wales and dragged everyone, kicking and screaming, with him into buying into his vision."

This is why Warnock and Cardiff are so suited. "Most football clubs aspire to be these passing teams, playing sexy football, but the Cardiff fanbase doesn't really respond to that. "They'll cheer for a big tackle as much as a goal sometimes, they love players who play with heart and soul – that's why they responded to Sol Bamba so much."

Booth concurrs: "So many clubs think they've got a divine right to, or an illustrious history of, passing and expansive football, but Cardiff fans almost accept where they are in the grand scheme of things."

Opposition managers and fans are left wondering how they've managed to lose against Cardiff after having 70% possession. Warnock will tell you it's all about playing the game well, while his critics will say he's not playing it properly. Who cares about critics, though? Not Cardiff fans and certainly not Warnock. Winning football games is all that truly matters.

Lots of things made Warnock's appointment a good match for City: his age, his knowledge of football, his background. Keith Morgan, football finance expert and chairman of Cardiff City Supporters Trust, says this experience was as important as anything in making his time a success, but also being instrumental in bringing the different parts of the club together again. "Neil Warnock was someone I used to hate when he brought other teams to play us," he tells me. "They call him a Marmite manager – you love him or hate him, and that's right."

Warnock has the knack of making the best of what he has. "I thought he would be ideal to get the most out of limited resources at the club – limited both financially and in terms of players," says Morgan. "He has always had a record of getting the most out of players to make them better. So when he came I thought he had the right skillset to get the most out of what was a limited squad.

"He's also at an age where if he thought he couldn't get on with Vincent Tan or Ken Choo in terms of what he was trying to do, then he could just turn around and walk out. Getting the likes of Junior Hoilett and Sol Bamba in was also key as he had already convinced them of his skills and his management style, therefore he had allies in the dressing room." These were the foundations for Warnock's Cardiff City rebirth.

He immediately brought in players who both respected him and brought essential qualities to the team – leadership, enthusiasm, confidence, pace. Bringing these players to the dressing room as soon as he arrived put Warnock's mark on the team. Fans loved them straight away, especially Bamba who – even after only 90 minutes against Bristol City – showed that he was a man who didn't give up.

"We were missing a leader for years after Mark Hudson left," says Leighton. "Everybody knew that. When Bamba played in the first game at home there was instantly a leader on the pitch. That leadership had been missing for so long and Warnock did something about it straight away."

The way Warnock talks, how he behaves on the touchline, the unguarded celebrations with fans after a victory, changed things at Cardiff, instantly. So did even the simple act of signing two out-of-work footballers who he knew well.

They had assets the squad was badly missing. Most importantly, they helped foster a new bond between the players. Tan benefitted from this, too. Were fans gradually forgiving him for past mistakes? If they hadn't yet, they would by the end of the next season.

It's difficult to get a clear answer to just how and why Warnock was the man to properly unite Cardiff City – and redraw Tan's relationship with fans in the process. His character, his honesty, the way he talks, the way he behaves on the touchline, the way he celebrates with supporters after a victory with that punch in the air. Even the simple act of signing two out-of-work footballers who he knew well, changed things instantly.

They had assets which the squad was badly missing. Maybe, most importantly, they were characters needed to help Warnock foster a new bond between the players. Tan benefitted from

49

this, too. Were fans gradually forgiving him for past mistakes? If they hadn't by that stage, they would have by the end of the next season.

"When Trollope was appointed it felt like Vincent Tan had lost interest," comments Leighton. "We'd had a mishmash of different managers, with different styles, and with an unbalanced playing squad. The atmosphere was totally, totally dead. We thought we were in trouble. I honestly can't think of any other manager in world football who could've come in and not just built a winning way on the pitch but would have also taken Vincent Tan and the fans with him."

For two-and-a-bit seasons, supporters had suffered the "You've sold your history" chants from opposition fans; they'd done the protests and signed the petitions. Cardiff felt more broken than just a club arguing about the team kit. There had been the managerial mishaps and the chaotic transfer choices. There were moments, too, when it felt as though the owner didn't care anymore, that nobody was really bothered how well or badly things went. A virus of ambivalence had infected everything. Not even the fans, renowned around the country for their passion, had the energy any more.

Nobody, really, was even that bothered when the Bluebirds went down from the Premier League in 2014 – as Morgan explains: "Last time we went up we were so disjointed and there was so much infighting. I didn't particularly mind that we got relegated, I didn't like the fact that we weren't all pulling together. This time it feels better. We're united."

Warnock's impact was immediate. It helped that his first match was a win against local rivals. It helped that one of his new signings scored. It helped that he spoke in a way which endeared him to fans.

When Warnock joined Cardiff he was 68. His wife, Sharon, had been diagnosed with cancer the year before. Warnock being out of work and Sharon recovering at home, gave him an unexpected new zest for football – while at the same time, providing perspective on the ups and downs of the game.

He's loved recounting the story to reporters. Sharon, in need of calm, found her husband was getting in her way and encouraged him to take the job at Rotherham. In an interview with the *Western Mail*'s Chris Wathan at the end 2016, Warnock was unapologetic about Sharon's influence on his decisions. "She's so important to me," he told Wathan. "She's gone through 12 months of hell and it does put things into perspective; football is important, not the be-all and end-all, not when you go through something like that. It has been difficult but she's come out the other side, battling back, and she's dealt with it better than me. If I sneeze I go to the doctors but I think all blokes are like that, like wimps, whereas women tend to bear up."

It was a revealing piece about Warnock, about what drives him – about why he was motivated to make his time at Cardiff worth it. It was also an admission that, at 68, he could no longer do everything as he might have done when he started out in management.

As the season went on, Cardiff's momentum built. Warnock, along with his trusted coaching assistants, Kevin Blackwell and Ronnie Jepson, was injecting new enthusiasm into the City squad. Form before Christmas, though not relegation standard, was indifferent compared with the rest of the season, with wins becoming easier and easier. Four wins out of six in January, three out of five the next month – including a thumping 5-0 win over Warnock's old club Rotherham – pushed City closer to the play-off places.

The Bluebirds also beat Leeds – great rivals ever since the 2001 FA Cup clash at Ninian Park – at Elland Road. Normal service had resumed. That winter's transfer window was used sparingly by Warnock, there remained a reluctance to spend much with nothing to play for, but utility man Greg Halford from Rotherham, goalkeeper Allan MacGregor from Hull City and striker Ibrahim Meite from non-league Harrow, were all added to the squad.

There was no need to splash out on a striker that January – we had Zohore, who had now found his form and was displaying a talent few realised he had. Warnock himself admitted as much. He wasn't going to waste time and energy overspending in a market notoriously biased towards the seller. Zohore was suddenly a player willing and ready to take on any defence in the division and he ended the season as top scorer with 12 goals. His transformation was the on-the-pitch embodiment of the Warnock effect the press had come to love writing about.

In an article for *WalesOnline* in February 2017, when he assessed Rotherham's record when Warnock was in charge, Booth pointed out just how that transformation manifests itself in results. Warnock saved them from relegation, when they were seemingly down and out by the turn of the year. 'Cardiff, like the Millers were last season, have been invigorated by Warnock,' he wrote. 'The Bluebirds are now in the top half, with six wins from their last nine games, having claimed two sizeable scalps inside a week. Leeds United and Derby County have both been vanquished, now Warnock's side must take on the mantle of 'favourites' once again, but it was the same underdog 'blood and thunder' ethos that allowed Warnock to produce a miracle at the New York Stadium last season.'

Warnock that season didn't perform a miracle, but he brought confidence to a club where it had been leaching away. Supporters nagged by a subconscious self-doubt, now had their identity patched back together after having it destroyed a few years before. Players who'd dithered, heads down, confused about how they should play after so many managerial changes, and wondering what they were doing there. The owner, having been taught a lesson in football fandom, had been forced into a rare U-turn on a decision. This was the club Warnock had come into: drifting and aimless. Lower league obscurity a real prospect. He admits this is exactly the sort of test that he loves.

"A lot of people almost fell out of love with it all," says Leighton about life at City before Warnock. "We all thought we were going to plummet through the divisions. It's hard to put your finger on it. The thing I liked when he came in was, for the first time in a long time, we had a manager who seemed to really connect with the fans. What he said was almost like a fan speaking. In interviews, a lot of managers who would try to pull the wool over the fans' eyes. Neil Warnock is so honest and fans really respond to that."

Fans at other clubs might laugh at that description of him, but that's the thing about the Warnock effect. When he's at your club he's as honest as they come, but he'll throw grenade after grenade of doubt at opponents with his cunning and double-speak – and it usually works. This is the 'Marmite manager' at his best. Uniting his tribe, but dividing and confusing everyone else.

Sarah McCreadie argues that Tan's decision to bring back blue and his appointment of Warnock meant that "unity has been restored". She explains: "The main thing was that we had to go back to blue and then Neil Warnock sorted out the rest on the field – it's a perfect coming together of a manager and a club. Our identity as a football club has been restored and as a team it has been instilled. Nobody has ever seemed to like us very much and now even more so with Warnock leading us – and I love it. No matter what happens next season we're going to enjoy every second. I can't wait to get to the Premier League, have a great time and piss everyone off. I love this club."

As the 2016-17 season went on, City continued to enjoy more wins and draws than they had to suffer defeats. The chance of a play-off spot had been lost before Warnock arrived though, and they paid for the dreadful start to the season under Trollope. The consistency wasn't quite there either, with defeats being inflicted a little too regularly for the club to have a real shot at the play-offs.

There was, though, the nucleus of something special to come – Warnock already believed his team would be in with a chance the following season.

"We're all singing from the same hymn sheet," Warnock said of the club as the end of the campaign came into sight. "I don't think I have been unreasonable and I think they are desperate to do well – Vincent, [chairman] Mehmet [Dalman] and [chief executive] Ken [Choo] – we all want the same thing," he told BBC Wales.

In the final game of the season, City walloped Huddersfield – who went up via the play-offs. With a new two-year contract signed in February, Warnock knew the magnitude of his achievement – and the challenge ahead. "When you go to a club second from bottom, it's fair to say it wasn't in a very good situation when I arrived," he told reporters after that final game.

"I actually had interviews at Nottingham Forest and Blackburn Rovers so I wonder what they are thinking today now we've finished in the top-half. I had good interviews but they went elsewhere so that's Cardiff's gain. I think I've turned the club around; I don't think it's the end of the job, but I do think we're moving forward in the right direction on and off the field."

Red Adair was back in football, doing the thing he did best: putting out fires.

5

A Quiet Summer?

"This is the pinnacle for me. Cardiff's such a big club and I don't think even Cardiff realise how big a club they could be."

Neil Warnock

Neil Warnock's summer of 2017 was undramatic and understated. There was little fuss made about the business he was doing. It was busy, yes, but there was nothing to really trouble the football writers or messageboard users. More political disquiet, thanks to a snap general election called by Prime Minister Theresa May, was taking the attention on social media anyway.

City fans might well have wondered about the players Warnock was bringing in. Neil Etheridge on a free from Walsall. Who was this keeper? Give us David Marshall back! Nathaniel Mendez-Laing, another free transfer, from Rochdale. A winger destined for a year in the reserves, surely? Who was Callum Paterson, a crocked full-back from Hearts who wasn't fit enough to kick a ball when he signed? Nobody had even heard of Loïc Damour – another free transfer – or the club he was signed from: Bourg-en-Bresse Péronnas. Who? They weren't even in *Ligue 1*.

May had her work cut out convincing voters to give her the mandate to deliver Brexit, and on June 8, she could only secure enough seats to form a government with the help of Ulster's DUP. Warnock, meanwhile, would have had *his* work cut out trying to convince fans that these players would lead a promotion assault if supporters hadn't fully bought into what he was building at Cardiff – but through his very actions, they already had.

The transfers, actually, were the antidote to the extravagant spending of the past. What do City fans want? Players who'll give everything when they pull on the blue jersey. What had Warnock already given them? Sol Bamba, Junior Hoilett and a first team transformed in demeanour and results. Supporters trusted him. They might not have heard of Damour, Mendez-Laing, Etheridge, or even Danny Ward – signed for £1.6m from Rotherham – but these were Warnock players, so they were bound to have something about them.

Then there were the pre-season preparations. Not a glamorous tour of the Far East, or North America, or even some warm weather training camp in Europe enjoyed by City squads of recent years. Not even Frank Burrows-style trips to Scotland or Ireland – instead, City took the short trip to Devon and Cornwall to play a couple of games against Bodmin and Tavistock, and train in the Cornish countryside close to Warnock's home (his "little bit of heaven"). It was here that he was to mould a team of winners who'd soon be on a record-breaking start to the season.

WalesOnline's Dom Booth followed the squad down the M5 and along the winding A30 through some very picturesque landscapes. "It was really unusual," he explains. "Staying in hotels down in Tavistock and Plymouth and travelling to sleepy villages. It started with Taff's Well, which itself was a bit different. "Warnock really did want to take it to the people and for the players to be distracted by fans, signing things and have their pictures taken. From a team perspective it was about Warnock gelling a team, bringing the squad closer together and to the fans. From a media perspective it was something we hadn't seen before. He wasn't trying to make commercial revenue out of pre-season, he wasn't even trying to test his players from a footballing perspective – he just wanted them to have a nice run out and get to know one another."

The mythology of the promotion year was already beginning to ferment. 'Remember that season Cardiff City were promoted? That great season when they came from nowhere to finish second in the Championship? Well, before the season started their players went on a trip to Cornwall where they played ping-pong and had a barbecue at the manager's house.'

Booth argues that Warnock's tactic of bringing players to intimate grounds with few facilities was part of the plan, of the continued diplomatic mission to bring the club back together, of the need to give players some grounding in reality. There was no getting away from autograph hunters or selfie sticks, though. "It was lovely to have a week down in Cornwall, there were no facilities, there was no Wi-Fi – things you're used to when you're on the road as a reporter," Booth says. "It was proper 'back to basics' stuff and after each match was over you'd walk onto the pitch and interview Warnock. It was totally different. It wasn't China or Dubai like some Premier League clubs travel to.

"They went down to a golf resort called St Mellion, where the players could have a game of golf or table tennis or whatever. On one day, Warnock turned up – at an open training session at Duchy College – in his 1970s Aston Martin, before the players and staff were all invited back to his house for a barbecue. "Against Bodmin, the bus wouldn't fit into the football club's car park so they simply parked the bus away from the ground and the players walked the final 50 yards through the Cornish countryside to the small stadium – chatting to fans, signing programmes and having their photographs taken. It was all very relaxed and friendly, even though there were probably more Cardiff fans than locals at the match."

Truthfully, such modest preparation for the season led to only a few die-hards believing much would happen when the competitive games began – but Warnock and his backroom staff knew better.

They spoke of a "special feeling" about the squad after watching them develop together in those days and weeks leading up to August.

It was enough to prompt Sean Morrison to commit to the club and turn down a transfer to Sheffield Wednesday, who'd submitted bids of £5m for the Bluebirds captain. They wanted him badly, but Morrison had more of a desire to be a part of this Warnock dream.

Warnock knew just how important the pre-season tour was to his side's achievements. He tells me his players thought he'd had one too many, when, as he hosted a small gathering at his home, he spoke of this feeling he had about the side's prospects. "During pre-season in Cornwall I said to them, 'Lads, I can sense something special. We've got something going here and if we get in the play-offs we can definitely go up – because I'm quite good at the play-offs!'

"Sean Morrison came to me afterwards and said, 'Have you been on the Champagne?'

"He thought I'd been drinking – nobody thought we could get in the play-offs – but I knew if we could recruit properly, I could tell there was something special happening. We were fortunate and brought in some cracking lads in the summer. It's been a pleasure to prove the doubters wrong," he says: "They're such a good group."

City's first pre-season game before the adventure down west, was a short drive up the A470 to Taff's Well, a village just north of the capital where 'the valleys' begin, for a game against the Welsh League side and played in the shadow of the Garth mountain. Warnock's travels around south Wales, meeting fans at various sports and social clubs, prompted him to arrange a friendly against a smaller club.

"When I go out into the valleys I don't just do that to get a few 'well dones'," he explained to *WalesOnline*, "I go out to communicate with all the local people – and that's why I go to Taff's Well. I've always gone to a local team to start (pre-season) with. You get critics but it brings the players down to earth. I had someone saying to me, 'Do you want to get changed at [Cardiff City Stadium]?' But I said, 'Do I hell?' I want to change at Taff's Well, in their dressing room and let the players have a look at it – because they might be playing there if it wasn't for me!"

Warnock had knocked on the door of Taff's Well's Rhiw'r Ddar ground with his driver – who was from the area – telling shocked chairman Liam Edwards that he "wanted to play against a local grassroots side and get the community involved".

The friendly would raise money for two charities which meant much to Warnock – Cancer Research UK and Velindre Cancer Centre – and to give Taff's Well a much-needed boost to its cash flow for the rest of its season. The Bluebirds won 1-0 on a warm July evening, but the result had little relevance. Pre-season matches rarely do.

Mendez-Laing, Etheridge and Damour were all given a run-out and nearly 3,000 turned up to watch a strong City squad take on the part-timers. "It sounded clichéd but Warnock really did take it to the people," says Booth. "Players stopped and signed things for fans. It was a very open environment and it was bizarre to see really recognisable players in these little grounds."

This is what Warnock wants football to be about – it's about winning games and achieving things, like promotion. Yes, it has to be, but it's also about people connecting with clubs, with the game, with players and managers. He's not afraid – like many managers are – of speaking to fans and meeting them face to face, and he wants his players to enjoy the warm bonds with those who pay good money to watch them play every week. He wants players to show their humility and he wants fans to appreciate his players as people, not superstars. That's why the trip to Devon and Cornwall, and the visit to Taff's Well, was so important. It was giving players a grounding, a context for their role – and duty – as Cardiff City players.

"By the time they went to Cornwall, they'd already signed a couple of players – Etheridge and Mendez-Laing – who we assumed would not figure much," Booth says. "But he was putting them up for the media as well and that was it, from that point onwards he was telling his players: 'we are one group'.

"Loïc Damour came in from France and here he was signing autographs for Cardiff City fans who'd never heard of him. It must have been a completely alien experience for the player. Warnock was very keen for him to chat to the press after the Bodmin game and, although Damour didn't feel confident enough to speak in English with the media at that point, you could sense that the squad felt united and harmonious. Even though they had issues with Lee Tomlin later on in the season and they had injuries as well, the tour served them well when those injuries hit, because people who went down to Cornwall felt a part of it and were ready to step in and do a job."

It was the week in Cornwall which really helped bind the squad. If building fitness, rather than winning games, was the premise for the training camp, it was even more important in creating and harnessing that abstract quality of camaraderie among the players.

This has been one of the defining distinctions of Warnock's style of management: establishing a bond in the group he's managing. One of the principal figures in influencing this ideal is one of Warnock's City predecessors: Len Ashurst. It was Ashurst who opened Warnock's thinking to the importance of team spirit and it being sparked by the manager.

In 1972, as a player with Ashurst's Hartlepool, Warnock and his teammates were sent on a pre-season overnight hike in the north Yorkshire countryside – in an exercise led by the team's fitness coach, ex-Commando Tony Toms – and forced to sleep rough with only a sleeping bag for comfort. In his autobiography, Warnock speaks of Ashurst, who took City back to the old Division Two in 1982-83, as having a 'fantastic ability to make everyone feel confident'.

When he joined Torquay in 1993, with the task of saving their league status, the first thing he did was take his squad of players out to a nightclub in the town with the threat to fine anyone who went home earlier than 1am. The team went on to win their next game and Warnock prevented the Gulls from going down.

At Notts County, before a big FA Cup fixture – a fifth round tie against Manchester City – in 1991, it snowed heavily. Instead of training in those conditions, Warnock bought a load of sledges and got his players to race each other down the slopes of a Nottingham park. They went on to beat Man City, of course.

It might sound contrived to anyone used to working in more conventional jobs, but in football, a sense of togetherness is vital if a team is to have any hope of doing well, and the trip to Devon and Cornwall was another example of his efforts to build solidarity.

City's first game of the tour was against Tavistock. It ended in a thumping 7-2 win for the Bluebirds. Portentously, Mendez-Laing scored twice and Kenneth Zohore was another on the scoresheet. It could have been an even bigger victory but City slowed the tempo down after half-time. Next, onto Bodmin and another win, this time 3-1 to City – before the proper football test, at Plymouth Argyle and another success for the Bluebirds who beat the Pirates 1-0, with Zohore scoring the winning goal. City's under-23s were along for the ride too, playing games against St Austell and Bideford while the senior players were rested.

After returning to Cardiff, Warnock prepared his new squad for two final friendlies before the Championship opener: a solitary 2-1 defeat, away at Shrewsbury, before a home game against Scottish side Livingstone, and another victory – 4-0.

Despite the consistency, despite the wins and the signings, fans didn't have total confidence in prospects for the season ahead, but Warnock did: "I do still get the buzz and I owe that to Sharon, my wife," he said. "With the medical problems that she had, that brought a lot of things into perspective, but the Cardiff fans have been fantastic. I got my zest back and my passion and I didn't think I could get that really. This is the pinnacle for me. Cardiff's such a big club and I don't think even Cardiff realise how big a club they could be."

The influence of Warnock's wife on his career and the decisions he makes is massive. Not only had she pushed him back into management when the Rotherham job came up, she was his most trusted confidante, advising him on all sorts. Warnock admits it himself, few men in his position are honest enough to admit the influence of their partner – less extol it in the way he does. He could hardly wait for the season coming up.

James Leighton was one of the minority, it was definitely a minority, of Bluebirds who thought this could be the year. "That first season, I remember telling my friends who weren't convinced when he came in and we were fighting relegation, that I could see us doing something and going for promotion," he says. "In the end it was a season too early.

"Then, over the summer, the bookies didn't have us down for doing anything and I couldn't understand it. I thought something big was growing there. We had an identity that we hadn't had before," he explains. "The transfer policy up until then had been a bit haphazard, with different managers bringing in players to suit their playing styles. As soon as he came in we had an identity, we started bullying teams and I liked that. Up until then, other teams had been coming to our ground and bullying us. I loved knowing other fans hated us and accused us of bullying, it meant we were doing something right."

What made that summer different? There had been one big name signing just before City departed for Cornwall: Lee Tomlin, signed from rivals Bristol City, who'd scored in that first game under Warnock the previous October. He was an attacking midfielder, a player with the creative spark missing from the team – especially now that Peter Whittingham had left.

Whittingham, signed from Aston Villa in 2007, had become the central player and a great servant for City for a decade. Although his left foot no longer scored as many goals as it had, he still provided much-needed quality from corners and free-kicks – a crucial asset in a Neil Warnock team. Yet, as the 2016-17 season drew to a close, it looked clear that he wasn't part of Warnock's vision for his new Cardiff team. He simply didn't have the legs to do the running and chasing the new boss expected. There was no way he'd be the first name on the team sheet as he had been under Warnock's predecessors and, with his contract up and no chance of him being offered terms to make him want to stay, Whittingham inevitably left as the season ended.

So Warnock, needing creativity, signed Tomlin who said he was "absolutely buzzing to be at the club and looking forward to getting started". Tomlin exuded the confidence Warnock had about City that summer – he probably knew he'd also be annoying fans at his old club too. "I want to get back to the Premier League and I feel I can do that here," he told *iFollow Cardiff City*. "I know a lot of the lads here already, which makes things even easier for me ahead of travelling down to Cornwall next week."

Neil Warnock added: "Lee reminds me of Adel Taarabt who I had at QPR. He's always a threat when he's on the ball and you're never quite sure what he's going to do, but I'm hoping I can get the best out of him here. There's a lot more to come from Lee. His creativity is second to none and we want to give him the platform to use that. This is the right atmosphere for him to revel in."

Warnock is a creature of habit, and he's superstitious. Since his move to Cornwall with Sharon when he was manager of Plymouth Argyle in 1995, he has taken his teams to train at Duchy College and play warm-up matches against local teams.

Another pre-season in Cornwall in 2018 was all about keeping the players "humble", says chief executive Ken Choo, before the Premier League season – egos need to be kept in check with dirty towels and showers that don't work.

In terms of football, there was little evidence of just how well Cardiff would do the following season. How can you gauge a team's ability after they've played Tavistock, even though they were reigning South West Peninsula Premier League champions.

What had we learned about this side and its chances of doing anything in the coming months? Well, we learned that the players are real people, that they enjoy being a part of a community and that footballers are not, entirely, egotists who care only for themselves and their bank balances.

The needs of Cardiff City being different to those at his other clubs, meant this trip was a part of the efforts to rebuild the club. Project Unity was still a massive part of Warnock's job. If that was an aim, then it was an ongoing success.

"The connection with the fans and the players and the manager is so special and something we haven't had for a long, long time," explains Sarah McCreadie. Fans were connecting emotionally with the team in a way that they had not done for years, and it helped establish a sense of anticipation for every match. Each 90 minutes meant something.

"This was a season," McCreadie continued, "that no matter where I was watching or listening, I felt every kick of the ball. I completely adore our players, with their big hearts and how they all seem to be ten feet tall with the ball glued to their feet. I've always felt proud to support Cardiff, and especially so this year. The team displayed spirit, character, unity and a swagger that to me felt so unmistakably 'Cardiff'."

Maybe other pre-seasons in Warnock-led teams were also about team togetherness, but this one was about so much more. It was about the club itself, he was instilling a sense of Cardiff-ness. A sense of a real belonging.

There was also a sense that the players were benefitting from this new approach in their performances. It may be tough to work out just how well – or badly – you're going to do from your summer friendlies, but you can see the players who look as though they'll be blessed with good form.

Joe Ralls, the midfielder who'd come through the ranks after joining as a youth player from Farnborough, was beginning to show that he had more about his game than the groan-prompting, sideway pass merchant identified by his critics. Underrated by most and unrated by far too many fans for much of his career up to Warnock's arrival, something had started to spark in Ralls at the end of 2017. Summer friendly team formations, transfer moves and selections, hinted that Warnock was going to entrust the young player with more responsibility. The team wasn't being built around him – that wouldn't be a Warnock thing to do – but he was going to be an essential element in the side.

Then there was Zohore. The manager had made it clear he didn't want to sell him, putting on him a ludicrous price tag – around the £20m mark – to put off any bidders. Hull and Brighton were most keen on the player, but Warnock wanted more than the £17m they'd offered. Zohore's agent claimed the player was being watched by Everton, too, who were "showing strong interest".

Darryl Powell told Danish tabloid *BT* that Brighton were turned away by both Zohore and Cardiff. Warnock was, again, the crucial factor in this. "Kenneth is very proud of everything Cardiff manager Neil Warnock wants," Powell said. "The manager sees a great star in Kenneth, and so I think the board and owners in Cardiff are really happy with Kenneth, [who] has an incredibly mature approach to it and respects his manager."

You could hardly have imagined this fevered transfer speculation about Zohore 10 months earlier – similarly the rumoured interest in Morrison by Sheffield Wednesday. The manager had made clear just how important he felt Zohore was to City's chances of being competitive in the season to come.

His statements had placed public pressure on the club's owner, chief executive and chairman to back him and keep the

Dane at the Cardiff City Stadium. "If I'm to have any chance, he won't be going anywhere," he'd told reporters that summer. It must have been tempting for them to accept the offers coming in, but with the peace between the club and its fans still fragile, supporting Warnock's position was the politically astute thing to do.

The last bits of transfer business were being done through August, Omar Bogle signed from Wigan Athletic for £700,000, while popular winger Craig Noone's time at Cardiff came to an end and he was sold to Bolton Wanderers. Two more additions were made on the last day of August – loan signings Liam Feeney, a winger from Blackburn Rovers, and Craig Bryson, a busy midfielder and Scotland international from Derby County.

By shipping out the dregs of the past – Tom Adeyemi, Adam le Fondre, Emyr Huws, Jordan Blaise, Idriss Saadi and Rickie Lambert – Warnock had quickly done what his predecessors could not, and the summer transfer window represented something new and potentially special for the Bluebirds.

Warnock has always been adept at starting afresh, he's done it at every club he's managed – from his time at Gainsborough Trinity onwards. He's spotted problems, personalities which don't fit in or which don't represent his beliefs, and solved them. He was now doing this with a flourish at Leckwith.

Warnock was learning about the rapport between players and within the group. Everything he'd done that summer 2017 was done for a reason, yet nobody outside the club had really taken notice of what was going on. City were 9/1 with some bookies, with 14 other clubs at shorter odds, on going up the next season and 33/1 on being champions of the division. Leeds, Bristol City and even Brentford all had better promotion odds. SkyBet had the Bluebirds at 6/1 to go down.

That wouldn't have bothered Warnock. He delighted in the fact that nobody fancied his side for promotion, his quiet summer of free transfers and expeditions to rural Cornwall mattered little to commentators. It was meant to, but Warnock knew something was happening. Even he was about to be surprised by just how big that something was, though. Cardiff City's season was about to begin: in style.

6

Hot Streak

"I knew this was going to be a special year while watching us play Aston Villa off the park, early on at home. It was a joy to watch us. From then on I was telling everyone we were going up."

Sarah McCreadie

There's a collection of clubs which form a cornerstone, bedrock, foundation of English football. They're overshadowed by the colossuses of the game, you know them well: Manchester United, Liverpool, Arsenal and in recent times Chelsea and Manchester City; but without them those big clubs would not be able to thrive. They have fleeting moments of success, periods when these teams think they've finally made it for good, but they invariably drift back to where they've mainly played.

They're teams like Crystal Palace, Norwich City, Nottingham Forest, Leicester City, Queens Park Rangers, Portsmouth, Charlton Athletic. Some have ideas of grandeur – Bristol City, Sunderland – some have rich histories when football glory was won in different eras – Preston North End, Burnley. English football would not be what it is without them.

They all share the common features of consistent attendances, decent grounds, and hopes of rejoining the very top class in the game, but they have, for most of their existence, been playing in the Championship (under whatever guise); the lower reaches of the top flight; or, when things are bad, in the bottom divisions. There, they flounder for a few years, looking and feeling completely out of place until a manager or owner or both drags them back up to their 'natural standing' in the world. Cardiff City are one of these.

When the Bluebirds first joined the Football League in 1920 it looked like they were destined to be among the big clubs. By 1924 they were runners up when Huddersfield Town won the league title, losing out on a goal average margin of just 0.024. By 1925, they'd reached their first FA Cup final where they lost to Sheffield United. Captain Fred Keenor lived up to his promise to return to Wembley when City were back in 1927, beating Arsenal 1-0.

The 1920s remain City's greatest era and the ultimate decade of false dawns. There was so much promise of a bright and successful future. The decline from that, which arrived – probably not coincidentally – with the Great Depression, was as quick and surprising as its rise into league football.

From then on Cardiff City has had good times (promotions, cup runs, spells back in the top division); some very dark times (relegations, administrations, empty stands) – and plenty of forgettably non-descript ones too (thank goodness for the play-offs for dangling the carrot of promotion in front of us during even the most drab of years).

Mostly, however, they've been a second tier side, with dreams of greatness, labelled a 'sleeping giant' but often struggling to prove deserving of that epithet.

The Ninian Park of 1920s manager Fred Stewart was pretty much the Ninian Park of 21st century boss Dave Jones. A few rudimentary changes were made in the intervening decades (roofs, seats, extensions, demolitions) but structurally it was a near-century-old legacy of the Bluebirds' soaring, Roaring Twenties.

It's against this history that City's start to the 2017-18 is measured. In the context of mostly average seasons – when even the finest successes have been inconsequential to, say, the record of Bob Paisley's Liverpool or Sir Alex Ferguson's Manchester United – a run of wins in August is always likely to break records.

Clubs like Cardiff City simply don't go on streaks that 'set the division alight' early on. They're meant to make up the numbers, while the bigger teams elbow everyone out of the race and win promotion by Easter.

Cardiff had never done better than winning their first two games of the season. For 118 years, City's teams have started off as they've meant to go on. It's an instructive statistic. Even celebrated promotion-winning sides had started off things with their squib dampened. In 1946-47, when a homegrown bunch of post-war talents romped to the Division Three South title, the first game was a 2-1 loss to Norwich which was followed up by a 3-2 loss to Swindon. It was only when Notts County visited Cardiff in September that the Bluebirds recorded their first win of the season. The Eddie May team of 1992-93 began with a 0-0 draw at Ninian Park against Darlington.

Neil Warnock's side of 2017-18 didn't just break the record, they smashed it. The Bluebirds won five in a row, they scored goals freely (10 in total), conceded very few (just the two and setting the standard for a miserly defence over the following nine months), they hit teams on the break, they excited. They were top of the division by the time August turned to September. Among those teams defeated were Wolves and Aston Villa: two favourites for promotion, two of the big spenders in the league.

It was form which was recognised by City's peers. Warnock was given the EFL Championship manager of the month award for August and, reflecting his terrific, goal-filled beginning to his City career, Nathaniel Mendez-Laing was awarded the player of the month.

Warnock explained that, along with goalkeeper Neil Etheridge, Mendez-Laing was one of his best signings: "Everything we wanted him to do, he did. It was great really, I got manager of month and he got player of the month that August. Speak to people at his other clubs, like Peterborough, they'd probably have said don't touch him, but I think he's come on so much and matured as well."

WalesOnline's Dom Booth believes the 2-1 victory at Wolves, eventual champions, that August remains the "best of the season". "Junior Hoilett and Nathaniel Mendez-Laing were electric in that game," he says.

Warnock warned others that his team would be hard to beat. Ahead of the match which ended City's streak (a 1-1 draw with Fulham), he gave an idea of what he thought a good season would be.

"I've said from day one, if we can be in the top four from the end of October then we've got a good chance of the play-offs. In the Championship you won't win every game, it's so difficult. It wouldn't be a shock if we lost all three games. We'll have to use the squad a bit. Bruno [Manga] isn't even back yet. We'll have to think carefully about selection."

Were supporters beginning to think this was it, as summer 2017 came to an end? "I knew this was going to be a special year while watching us play Aston Villa off the park early on at home this season. It was a joy to watch us," explained Sarah McCreadie. "I couldn't wait for the next game to come around so I could see those players again. From then on I was telling everyone we were going up."

The open top bus celebration through Cardiff after City secured promotion to the Premier League in 2013. Behind the smiles many fans had become disenchanted with the club following the rebrand to red. (© Wales News)

Left: Vincent Tan quickly became the focal point for the disharmony generated by the rebrand. (© Wales News)

Below: Piles of red scarves ready to be given away to Bluebirds fans. (© Wales News)

Malky Mackay (centre) with his coaching staff David Kerslake (left) and Joe McBride (right) on the training ground. (© Wales News)

Andreus Cornelius, an emblematic transfer flop from the Mackay era. (© Wales News)

A 3-2 win over Manchester City epitomised Cardiff's solid start to the season. (© Wales News)

Vincent Tan proudly watches his team. (© Wales News)

Ole Gunnar Solksjaer takes to the dugout against Swansea City. The Bluebirds were humiliated 3-0. (© Wales News)

The fans remained passionately pro-blue as protests continued through the 2013-14 season. (© Wales News)

Fraiser Campbell takes on Chelsea defender Branislav Ivanović in the final game of the 2013-14 Premier League season. Cardiff were relegated and in disarray. (© Wales News)

Despite City's indifferent form, Fabio impressed the fans with his skill, pace and committment. (© Wales News)

The following season started as badly as the previous one had ended, and it was only a matter of time before Solksjaer was sacked. The end came shortly after Cardiff's game against Norwich. (© Wales News)

Russell Slade looked more like an old-fashioned PE teacher than football manager. (© Wales News)

The crowds continued to drift away from the Cardiff City Stadium. (© Wales News)

The back-to-blue protests become more bold, with Tan firmly in the firing line. (© Wales News)

Empty blue seats contrast starkly with Peter Whittingham's red home kit. (© Wales News)

Just 4,194 turned up to watch Cardiff's FA Cup third round clash with Colchester, which the Bluebirds won 3-1 – Kenwyne Jones (top) among the scorers. The scoreline did little to deter fans from increasing their vociferous protests against the red rebrand. (© Wales News)

Siân Branson of fans' group Bluebirds Unite (top left) with City chairman
Mehmet Dalman (top right) at the press conference confirming the club was
to revert to its traditional blue colours. (© Wales News)

Dalman, flanked by chief executive Ken Choo and Vince Alm of Cardiff City
Supporters Club, was instrumental in persuading Tan to change his mind.
(© Wales News)

There was a carnival atmosphere at the Cardiff City Stadium for the Fulham game on January 10, 2015, as fans celebrated the return to blue. For most it was worth more than a fleeting appearance in the Premier League. (© Wales News)

"We'll always be blue" was sung with even more heart, and Cardiff fittingly won the game 1-0 thanks to a goal from Sean Morrison. (© Wales News)

As the 2015-16 season started Anthony Pilkington (top) was expected to lead the line in a forgettable season. Scott Malone, (bottom) the full-back signed from Millwall was another underwhelming Slade-era signing. (© Wales News)

Fabio's attacking verve was a bright spot amid some dull footballing moments in 2015-16. (© Wales News)

An empty Cardiff City Stadium remained devoid of atmosphere despite the return to blue. A spark was still missing. (© Wales News)

Dutch attacking midfielder Lex Immers' loan spell was a hit – but he could not replicate that form when he was signed permanently by Paul Trollope. (© Wales News)

Sean Morrison expresses his frustration during the match against QPR, a common emotion for the season. (© Wales News)

The Slade era was not all dour, there were wins and goals and a decent eighth place finish that season. Should history judge him differently? (© Wales News)

Slade was succeeded as manager by Paul Trollope, but the promising young coach could do nothing to improve results and was sacked just weeks into the 2016-17 season. (© Wales News)

Unveiled as the new Cardiff manager, Neil Warnock's infectious enthusiasm immediately changed the mood as he relished his first game against Bristol City. (© Wales News)

Sol Bamba, a new signing and a talisman of the new era of unity under Warnock, scores on his debut. (© Wales News)

Bamba made a positive and immediate impact. (© Wales News)

Warnock celebrates the 2-1 victory in his first game in charge at Cardiff. (© Wales News)

Junior Hoilett, another key signing during Warnock's first week, in action against Wigan. (© Wales News)

City started the new 2017-18 season in winning style and Nathaniel Mendez-Laing was a focal point for that attacking success. (© Wales News)

Sol Bamba (left) grew in presence while Junior Hoilett (right) was hitting the form of his career as Cardiff's winning streak went on through August. (© Wales News)

From "disgrace" to first name on the team sheet. Kenneth Zohore was a player transformed under Warnock. (© Wales News)

Joe Ralls was another to benefit from the management of Warnock, developing a directness in his game he'd only rarely shown previously. (© Wales News)

Captain Sean Morrison scored some crucial goals from set plays – arguably as critical as the solid defensive partnership he had with Bamba. (© Wales News)

Ralls showing his strength against Derby's Tom Huddlestone. (© Wales News)

Warnock's fist-pump salutes were becoming a trademark of the season. (© Wales News)

Mendez-Laing outruns former City loanee Tom Lawrence. (© Wales News)

Bamba was an attacking threat and scored key winning goals in tight matches. (© Wales News)

Lee Tomlin – a rare transfer flop for Warnock during his first 12 months at Cardiff. Signed from Bristol City he failed to make the impact fans hoped. (© Wales News)

Hull defenders struggled to contain Callum Paterson and utility player Greg Halford. Paterson's move to number 10 was critical in grinding out results. (© Wales News)

Joe Bennett's FA Cup red card against Manchester City seemed to spur the defender into a rich run of form in the second half of the promotion season. (© Wales News)

Kenneth Zohore's absence was felt during an injury hit season but new signing, striker Gary Madine, seemed to improve his energy. (© Wales News)

Paterson scores in the win over Sunderland in January 2018 – the beginning of a fantastic run of victories. (© Wales News)

Marko Grujić, on loan from Liverpool, celebrates with teammates epitomising the new sense of togetherness at Cardiff. (© Wales News)

Vincent Tan was back at the Cardiff City Stadium and wearing blue for the match against Reading, as fans looked forward to a historic afternoon. (© Wales News)

Kenneth Zohore sums up an afternoon of frustration on the pitch – but the result didn't matter as Fulham were beaten soundly by Birmingham City. (© Wales News)

Fans cannot hide their delight as promotion to the Premier League is secured, and this time it felt so different. (© Wales News)

Ecstatic Bluebirds, including City's general manager Ken Choo (bottom left) celebrate on the pitch. (© Wales News)

There were wild celebrations as blue smoke engulfed the CCS. (© Paul Bettridge)

Fan fashion expresses gratitude for Warnock's leadership. (© Dan Tyte)

What an unforgettable day for this young Bluebird, as fans celebrate with the 'ayatollah'. (© Wales News)

There were more than 30,000 City fans at the Reading match and most who could were on the pitch after the final whistle. (© Wales News)

Promotions are rare events for any fans, but this one was such a contrast to the bittersweet title-winning season of 2012-13. (© Wales News)

(© Paul Bettridge)

(© Paul Bettridge)

Vincent Tan was carried around the pitch on the shoulders of fans, then returned to the directors' box to celebrate with the manager who'd made City's return to the Premier League possible. (© Wales News)

Warnock and his team lift the promotion trophy. (© Wales News)

"You didn't believe we could do it!" Warnock's brilliant speech to supporters was a highlight of the city centre promotion party. (© Wales News)

Fans salute their team in the May sunshine. (© Wales News)

Owain Taylor pictured in 2014, aged 14, after the Bluebirds' relegation from the Premier League (top), and after the Reading match (below). He said he always believed his beloved City would win promotion back to the top division, and they did. (© Wales News)

Lifelong fan Philip Nifield echoed those thoughts: "I thought top 10 would have been good and we had an outside chance of the play-offs," he admits. "I think everyone would have been pleased with that, but he got us on a roll from the start."

The Villa game, another pick from that purple patch, was described as an "embarrassment" by their manager Steve Bruce, as Warnock savoured a match which provided the "reason why I'm in football" with its shots and saves and "oohs and ahhs".

"It's a rude awakening for us, very early again," said Bruce. "Arguably that's the biggest doing over I can remember having in the Championship. We didn't do enough of the basics. We looked fragile every time they broke on us." Cardiff embarrassing what was once one of the biggest clubs in England? This'll do nicely.

QPR manager Ian Holloway said it was the best Cardiff side he'd faced, after his team was beaten 2-1. "On the balance of play, that's as good a Cardiff team as I've seen," said Holloway. "Both wide men look back to their best, the big man (Zohore) is a handful, they were well organised, big and strong and played some good stuff, but I thought we did as well. I'm not too downhearted and disappointed."

Keith Morgan, of the supporters' trust, sums up just how important that opening run was to changing people's minds. "We thought we would be a mid-table team," he explains. "There are some big powerful clubs with lots of Premier League experience in the Championship. I don't think many fans thought we were strong enough to go up."

Five wins and 15 points. By the end of August, City had accrued as many points as they had at the end of October the previous year. The run also gave fans some false expectations of the way City would play for the rest of the season. This was direct football, yes. Long balls remained central tactically, with possession not an important statistic, but it was swashbuckling and exciting in the way that Warnock's teams had not been previously.

Wingers Hoilett, and the unknown Mendez-Laing, were crucial to this success – they would be for the remainder of the season, too. As Booth points out, Mendez-Laing had put in some impressive performances that month, after his move from Rochdale earlier in the summer, and scored four outstanding goals. Strong, pacey, quick-footed and an eye for the net – he was fast becoming the find of the Warnock era so far. He was the antithesis to the hoofball style ignorant critics assumed City played.

"Neil Warnock has this wonderful, overflowing passion that has breathed new life into this club and the fans love it," McCreadie added. "You can feel it when you go down to the stadium. He has created a team that play like they would do anything for him and each other. He's also given us an identity on the pitch, which is something we've really been missing – he has the players knowing exactly what they are doing.

"It's powerful, explosive football and anyone who says it's 'thuggish' has probably seen us play one game and has definitely never seen Nathaniel Mendez-Laing skilfully bamboozle anyone in his path on the wing. A lot has been said about this, but to achieve promotion with the little money he's spent is such an incredible achievement. He is no doubt the best Cardiff City manager I have known."

After seeing off Burton, Aston Villa, Sheffield United, Wolves and QPR, the wins ended with the draw at Fulham. Then came a 3-0 hammering at Preston North End.

Warnock took the blame for that one, putting it down to his team selection and reluctance to freshen up what had been a winning side. It was an early reminder for the manager to forget loyalty or duty when it comes to picking a side (he's spoken about it being his comeuppance before) and the wins and league leadership came along again as autumn opened up. "If Warnock's Cardiff were known for being direct, they had, at least, three styles of play within that directness," says Booth.

There's the gritty, determined, counter-attacking style with the ball moved from back to front with speed. Corners and free kicks are well-planned and practised and threaten the opposition goal. It's not theatre but it's effective and served City well for most of the season with plenty of points won in the final minutes of matches.

Then there was the scruffy-as-anything stuff, the games which left you wondering how on earth this side wasn't fighting relegation, let alone challenging automatic promotion. Such performances, thankfully, were rare – but they were reminders of the fine margins in tactics, team talks and motivated players.

The start of the season saw the best of it, maybe giving fans a mistaken sense of how this Bluebirds side would play for the rest of the campaign, but it was good, so easy to watch and the archetypal football Cardiff fans want to see: committed, simple, free-scoring, and lacking pretensions of being anything other than what it was – direct. There's the goal, now try and get the ball in it.

Wide play was key, Mendez-Laing's speed and Hoilett's guile setting up chances for Zohore and taking defenders with them to free up space for midfield runners. It's little wonder in this set-up that Hoilett was a top scorer and goals were spread out across the team. The improvement to Ralls – so noticeable over the second half the previous campaign – continued, meanwhile. "Ralls has been given the confidence, he's said you're my number one in midfield," says Booth. "Warnock told him, 'You are good on the ball', and he improved immeasurably. He has been given a bolt of confidence. The manager believes in him as a player and his reaction to it as been great."

Ralls was among the City scorers in those opening matches, his self-belief evident in the way he was spreading the ball around the pitch, setting up chances and hitting the back of the net too – his two goals in the first 10 games were in 2-1 wins at Wolves and Sunderland.

The statistics bear up the perception that Ralls improved under Warnock. Of Cardiff's main midfielders, he has the best numbers on passing and accuracy as well as key passes. He was, without question, the best central midfielder in the side as City mounted their challenge for a top two place. He now deserves to prove just how well he can do in the Premier League.

If all good things come to an end, then they do so in football with a lesson for those involved. The very best sides learn from those lessons. The average ones lurch back to mediocrity. There was no chance of that happening after Cardiff's minor slip-up (in the context of such a wonderful set of opening results) against Fulham and the sound defeat by Preston because, when Sunderland and Leeds were up next, City did not fail to show the character that Warnock demands from his side.

Sunderland were seen off with that win at the Stadium of Light, with Craig Bryson and Ralls scoring, but it was the top-of-the-table clash with Leeds which really made a statement about Cardiff's ambition for the season. A crowd of 27,000 packed into the Cardiff City Stadium and the Sky Sports cameras were there to broadcast it live. It was a game which was at times breathtaking in action and full of emphatic play. Anyone who says Warnock's Cardiff are a boring, lucky side should watch that match again.

It was won 3-1 with skill and flair, attack after attack, one-touch passing moves. It was a joy to watch, especially given who the opposition were. Hoilett's goal from 25 yards in the first half proved just how valuable a free transfer he was, while

Zohore's second, after the break, was a team goal full of midfield quality, overlapping runs and impactful passing.

More than anything though, it was Warnock's magic touch being played out on the pitch. It resonated with confidence and bravado. It had Sean Morrison running into the box to send the final ball across the goal. If Zohore hadn't scored, then Loïc Damour was ready to slide it in instead. Sol Bamba, asked to play an alien midfield role, looked imperious. Hoilett was unstoppable. Everyone in blue that night played with an energy and desire that hadn't been there under Slade and Trollope.

"This was a great night for us," beamed Warnock afterwards. "I was really pleased with the way we played and went about the job. The Warnock Way!" He was proud of the club and its "fantastic fans". "You pay to come and watch excitement and I thought there was excitement all over the place tonight."

He was right. Sky had had its money's worth out of City once again. There was also now a clear intent about what this season would be about. Even if, at this point, Warnock was being muted about his side's chances of even getting into the play-offs. The work on the reconciliation he'd put in was also showing its value.

"We worked very hard to get where we are," Warnock told the press after the Leeds match. "It wasn't straightforward. Off the field we were segmented, we weren't united. I know the staff around the training ground, and stadium morale was poor, but over 12 months we've done right. Who would have thought 27,000 all getting behind us like that. We have to enjoy the moment, while we're there."

Cardiff had won seven out of the first 10 matches of the season. They'd drawn two and lost only one. They were top of the table. If, as Warnock had commented, you're to judge football teams only once you're into October, then the Bluebirds looked certs to be at least in the play-offs come May.

Supporters, already scenting the faint prospect of promotion, were beginning to get excited – even the naturally pessimistic Cardiff crowd. The brand of football was not conventional eye-pleasing stuff, but it was providing positive results and continuing the fine form of the second half of the previous season.

"We had some of the lowest possession statistics in the division and fans at most clubs would not stand for it, they would be going crazy," says James Leighton, who says he always felt optimistic about the side's chances. Mostly, though, he was enjoying the style and substance of this Cardiff side's play. "At Cardiff we've had players like Graham Kavanagh, Stephen McPhail and Peter Whittingham, and when they've had the ball and tried to keep possession by playing it back or across the pitch – fans hated that.

"Watching us play this year has not always been pretty, but Cardiff fans love it. They want the ball forward early, they want to see the ball in the opposition penalty area. With Paul Trollope he wanted to build up from the back, but you'd end up playing 50 passes, lose the ball in your own half and then your defenders would end up chasing it to clear it and hit it up the field anyway. Warnock's football is fast and furious."

There were signs that the public was buying into the winning football. Attendances were creeping up, and the crowd for the Leeds game was better than any since a free-ticket offer brought in a record 28,863 to watch the Bluebirds take on Derby County in April 2016, when Russell Slade plotted his failed charge on the play-offs.

The average gate was above the benchmark 20,000 for the first 10 games, standing at 21,312, pushed up by the two bumper crowds for Villa and Leeds. The record run that August underpinned the season as a whole: it provided a reservoir of points, it put City in the top two where they stayed for virtually the rest of the season.

As important, was the confidence it gave Warnock's side. It instilled in players a belief and a fearlessness which they carried into every game. Sol Bamba was the embodiment of that fearlessness, and the rest of the first XI followed his example. "I've loved watching Sol Bamba and Sean Morrison this season. Sol Bamba hates losing, it's obvious, he's like a fan on the pitch," says Leighton.

Results reflected this as the team emerged from that breathless opening. Performances became more pragmatic as the autumn set in, the conditions changed and the demands of two games a week took their toll. City got through to December having won three out of their four matches in November.

Callum Paterson was now in the side having overcome the knee problem he'd brought with him on his arrival. He was scoring goals too. He'd come off the bench in City's 2-0 win over Brentford and looked every bit the lively player Warnock had promised. That was as a full-back.

He started the next game at Barnsley and scored. This time he was employed in a more offensive role, an attacking midfielder able to defend from the front, who had apparently unlimited energy and the capacity to score goals too. It made him probably the ideal number 10 in a Warnock side, and nothing like the player who was supposed to fill that role over the season, the gifted Lee Tomlin.

By the end of November, City were safely in second with Wolves leading the division. Warnock's team was being tested, with injuries having taken out Kenneth Zohore and Aron Gunnarsson. Important players though they were, Warnock had found capable replacements in Bryson, Loïc Damour and Paterson for Gunnarsson and Danny Ward and Omar Bogle for Zohore. The inexperienced Bogle often looked like the ideal back-up for the senior striker, his pace and scoring record when he did play showed he could do it.

Goals, then, were still coming, although the points were beginning to be ground out with more difficulty than they had previously been. This was not the convincing stuff that fans had enjoyed through August, it was a more conventional 'route one' style, but it still brought success and embedded the Bluebirds as promotion contenders. Even playing like this, they hardly looked like slipping up – it was almost as if they were holding back, keeping the energy in reserve with the tough winter months still to come.

From August to November, Cardiff City were imperious. Only one side – Preston – had found any flaws. Other defeats were by finer margins, like the Birmingham match which was lost 1-0, or moments of unfathomable mistakes, like the Omar Bogle red card at Bristol City, where Cardiff lost 2-1.

Most of the time, particularly when Zohore was missing, Cardiff were always *in* games, even when not *on* their game, with two useful centre-halves – often as good attacking opposition goals as they were at defending their own – who looked like they could grab goals from corners, long throws or free kicks. The big question was 'could City continue like this?'

The real challenge now for Warnock and his team was keeping this momentum up as the season headed into winter, and a run of matches concertinaed through the festive period are a test for every side. It was a stretch of wins and draws which largely secured promotion to the Premier League in 2012-13, the importance of December to promotion hopes, then, is enormous.

Despite Warnock's summer additions, keeping as many of his stars fit and able to play would prove another decisive element in maintaining the good form. With Zohore and

Gunnarsson already out along with others including full-backs Jazz Richards and Joe Bennett, ensuring the majority of the squad remained match-ready was a priority in building on the foundations that had already been laid.

Wins would be even more difficult if a key member of the team, say Sol Bamba or Sean Morrison, was missing for any spell of games. Warnock admitted that in previous years he'd have worried about their absence. Maturity had given him a broader perspective, though. "If you picked two players to put down first [on the team sheet], you'd pick those two [Zohore and Gunnarsson]," he told the BBC ahead of the Millwall match at the end of October. "I don't worry so much now. When I was younger it always seemed to be my best player who got injured and I used to panic and not sleep at night."

At the end of October, City defeated Ipswich Town – a side Cardiff have struggled to beat in recent Championship encounters – 3-1 at home. Hoilett, Bogle and Ward all scored. Ipswich had won the possession stats, but more tellingly, City had 19 shots on goal. The game could have been won by so many more.

The Bluebirds had been the form team in the division since Warnock's appointment and now he was leading this unfashionable club on an unlikely promotion attempt. A consistent December would cement their place as one of the Championship teams to beat. With winnable fixtures too, the form was surely Cardiff's to continue. Only something disastrous could undermine all the work that had been put in so far and throw an unwelcome wave of doubt over prospects for promotion.

7

The Blip

"There are going to be certain times in the season when players have got to give you that little bit more. You have got to get that bit more out of them yourself."

Neil Warnock

What makes a team a great one? Is it the manner of its victories? The victims it leaves in its wake? Is it its intensity? Its relentlessness? Is the fabric of its greatness its outstanding players? Its guile and flair? Or is it character? Is true greatness in a team defined by that team's ability to come back from defeat and setbacks? Greatness is all of these things and much more.

The quality which makes this Cardiff City side undoubtedly one of the club's all-time greats, is their ability to bounce back from disappointments – whether that's a goal, a defeat, dubious refereeing, or injury. Overcoming every difficulty thrown their way, they have shown underdog spirit in the purest of senses.

It's the quintessence of Neil Warnock's ethos. It was displayed time after time throughout the season. Whenever something went wrong, heads did not drop. Failings were made collectively and responded to without pause. It was why the best form of the season was preceded by the worst.

Warnock knew it was going to happen at some point. With his small squad made up of some absolutely key players, an injury crisis was bound to hit. Yes, the Cardiff City of 2017-18 is about the whole rather than its parts, but if – say – Kenneth Zohore, Sean Morrison, Aron Gunnarsson or Junior Hoilett were out of contention, then the absence would be keenly felt.

You could have probably pinpointed the time of year too – when the pitches start to wear and the games begin to stack up, before the transfer window opens so new recruits can freshen up a tiring dressing room. In one word: December. A month which tested everything Warnock and his staff had built so far, a month which triggered most pessimism, even raising questions about tactics and team selection.

Speaking to Warnock, he knows just how tough that time was, and just how much doubt it prompted among the supporters. He has no worries about telling you that. Fans were wondering if the fabulous start to the season was being undermined in a run of just a few games. The manager knew there were murmurings. Warnock knows too that if anyone can lead a group of players through indifferent form, then he is the one who can do it.

He tells me the importance of knowing how to get the best out of players – who to cajole, who to tell off, who to direct and who to empower with responsibility. Tactics might be essential – nobody could ever say that set pieces or an organised defence aren't intrinsic to Warnock's ability to win – but it's crucial, too, to work with a player's mind and appreciate that each one is completely unique. Warnock recognises how much of a strength his man-management is – he's the best at it in British football right now. "I think some clubs have about five members of staff for what I do – psychologists and whatever else. There are going to be certain times in the season when players have got to give you that little bit more. You have got to get that bit more out of them yourself."

All of his skill as a leader and psychologist would be needed as the Christmas break began. In fact, December itself started well, though results of the month's first three games disguised some mediocre performances.

City beat Norwich 3-1 on the first Saturday of the month, with Lee Tomlin playing a refreshingly key role in that match after coming off the bench for the second 45 minutes of the game. The first half, however, was as bad as any since Warnock arrived. The story of that game itself was a sign of things to come: bouncing back from failure. "I haven't done a half-time team talk like that since I have been at Cardiff, the last time I did something like that it went on YouTube!" he told BBC Wales, referring to an infamous dressing room rant filmed during his time at Sheffield United.

"I wish I could have made five substitutions at half-time, we were that bad. I couldn't see how we could be worse, but in the second half there were so many pluses. It's nice, we were at it right from the word go in the second half. Everyone contributed, including the fans."

A trip to Reading was next. A point was ground out, with City 2-1 down after a late Royals' goal. Give up after that? No way. It was Tomlin who rescued the Bluebirds with an injury-time equaliser. "I have to give the lads credit to rally and show resilience to pull it back from two goals down," said Warnock after that one: "we could have won by five," he added, characteristically bullish.

The next win, at home against Hull City watched by 18,000-odd, would be the last one for weeks. It was a 1-0 win. Sol Bamba the scorer. City, secure in second, were now just four points behind leaders Wolves. In the Friday press conference before Christmas, Warnock assured everyone that he was committed to Cardiff for this season, that he "wouldn't dream" of leaving midway through, and revealed he had found the enthusiasm to work the next one as well, whatever happened in the months to come.

Promotion? It was on. Crowds may still have failed to reflect this optimism (averaging below 20,000), but there was definitely a seed of thought that this was going to be memorable. Happy Christmas Cardiff City? Well, this is Cardiff City we're talking about.

The festive period is notoriously difficult. It has the power to make or break seasons with its matches played almost every other day. Sometimes being the best doesn't even come into the equation, it's how you stifle the opposition's attacking might, how you play to every limited strength to snatch whatever you can from the 90 minutes. The matches at the end of the period are rarely anything but scrappy. Luck plays its part in how you do – a good or bad referee can make the difference between a win or loss – so does fitness, as well as how threadbare or well-stocked your squad is.

When City went up under Malky Mackay it was Christmas which secured the Championship. That says something about the size of that squad and just how fit they were. The rest of that season was a stroll. In 2017-18, Christmas under Warnock was more a Cardiff City Christmas, with bank holiday promise and disappointments. The Boxing Day turkey and chips invariably, inevitably spoiled by those bloody players in blue. The reason for it? Undoubtedly injury problems as bad as at any time when Warnock had taken over. The impact of one missing player in particular would have massive consequences.

"We knew with the squad that we've got, we were going to get an injury situation," Warnock tells me. The situation saw

Zohore and Gunnarsson both out already. Gunnarsson's was the worst – his ankle again, but it was the injury to captain Sean Morrison, which would really hit.

Morrison was another incumbent whose career was stalling when Warnock arrived. Undoubtedly he could count among one of the "good lads" Warnock knew were at the club already, but one who needed some nurturing to turn into the player he could be, considering he'd been signed for a tidy sum from Reading a couple of years earlier.

Warnock gave Morrison the captaincy, told him he was a top player, and said he was the kingpin of his defence. Not just that, he was given a bit of freedom and confidence to go forward and score. With Morrison and Sol Bamba barging defenders and putting pressure on goalkeepers, City had an entirely new and effective means of attacking the opposition goal. So when Morrison limped out of the Reading game early with a muscle problem, it was the start of a dip in form which, at the end of the season could be seen a just a blip, but which, at the time, seemed like it could upset the Bluebirds' promotion chances.

Morrison's groin problem was arguably the greatest factor in City's poor performances. Other players were absent too, Craig Bryson and Anthony Pilkington (back in favour after looking as though he'd be on his way out of the club) were keeping the physios busy, while full-back Jazz Richards' season was one beset by fitness difficulties.

Missing now too was Danny Ward, a £1m signing from Rotherham, who was beginning to look busy and goal hungry before knee ligament damage brought his season to an end in December – with Zohore's unavailability because of his ankle problem, Warnock also had problems up front.

The injury crisis came just in time for the stacked-up football diary. The time of year when the hackneyed phrase "thick and fast" gets worn to death by soccer people. Cardiff's festive fixture list was: Bolton away on the 23rd; Fulham at home on Boxing Day; Preston at home the following Friday night; and QPR away on New Year's Day.

All those games were winnable. Fulham were a mid-table team, looking at that time as though they'd be going for the play-offs at most. Bolton were in the bottom three, and QPR were underperforming with their own relegation worries. Of all the games, it was Preston which looked the most difficult. The Lillywhites were winning games, sat just outside the play-offs in ninth and only 12 points behind Cardiff before Christmas.

Second-placed City's win-draw-win form going into it meant a four-point gap with Bristol City who were in third. It was a cushion at least. The anything-can-happen nature of games at this time of year with matches so compressed meant the table could read wildly different come January 2. The scene was set. City had an injury crisis and four games in 10 days. So much could change in such a short period of time.

Paul Bettridge has been a City fan since the mid-1980s. He speaks of the growing consensus, if it was one not really seriously talked about, that there was a possibility of Cardiff going up as winter drew on. "It was looking likely that we could be in with a chance of promotion," he says. "Then those four games happened and it was, 'Oh no, the wheels are coming off'. With the first two games, you held onto the optimism, but then the other two games came along and I thought – maybe we were going to be doing that Cardiff City thing – when everything goes wrong. The Fulham game was bad, and then Preston felt like we'd taken a step back after all the good stuff and the promise. I was even wondering if Warnock's magic was fading."

We know now that it wasn't, but Warnock says he could sense that feeling coming from the stands. Over a season of

46 matches, four games are almost inconsequential. In the noise of Christmas football, a bad string of fixtures can feel season-ending, however. It's little wonder that pessimism might have begun to creep in. Naturally, Warnock would go on to use this in his favour, as a motivational tool ("remember when they lost faith in you when we lost those games before? Well you went and showed them didn't you?" he'd tell his team).

First he'd have to drag his players through some of the most difficult games of the season, with only an FA Cup tie against Mansfield Town at the end of it for breathing space from the league. With Morrison out, it was up to Manga and Bamba to see off opposition attacks.

Zohore was being fast-tracked back to the first team, as Omar Bogle's early promise was wearing off.

Bolton beat City 2-0 at the Macron Stadium, Gary Madine (a major figure in the promotion story for good or ill) scoring one of Wanderers' goals from the penalty spot. Warnock disputed it, in typical style ("Deliberate handball? Come on!"), and had plenty to say about the referee's performance.

"When you come up against a side like Bolton, you need a strong referee and I think he was weak today. I thought some of the challenges were horrendous early doors and I think we've had more bookings than them," he said after the match.

Christmas Day did little to recharge the batteries. To everyone's relief, Zohore did return for the Fulham game (securing £25 from Warnock, who'd bet with him against it, for playing the full 90 minutes). His presence might have brought more balance, and given that vital outlet for those trademark long balls, but it wasn't enough to bring three points, or even one. Zohore scored that afternoon, but the 21,000 who watched were left bitterly frustrated by an uncharacteristic showing. The match was lost 4-2. Warnock too voiced his dissatisfaction, but as ever gave the loss his own positive slant.

This was the first home defeat of the season, but if anyone had told him – before the season started – his side would be unbeaten at the Cardiff City Stadium by Christmas he'd have been quite happy. Zohore, the talismanic forward, upon whose shoulders was heaped so much pressure after the summer of speculation, was back in the side and fully fit – Warnock had one eye on the bigger picture than just a few matches. "We lost, yes, but this must have been a good Fulham side to beat us at our place."

His assessment of the match was prophetic. The Fulham team was a damned good one, and their win at Cardiff arguably the starting point of an astonishing run which should, in any other season, have secured them automatic promotion, if not the Championship title itself.

This was no ordinary season, though, even by Championship standards. The Bluebirds were now out of the top two, replaced by Bristol City, and Tuesday's Boxing Day clash with Fulham was followed by a Friday evening one against Preston North End. If any team holds a curse over Cardiff then it's Preston. Who will ever forget that Dave Jones era match where the Bluebirds were wallopped 6-0 to put an end to any play-off hopes? It proved as problematic a game as it threatened to be.

Cardiff's performance was woeful. When this team looked bad, it looked really bad. Anyone seeing them play for the first time that night would be forgiven for wondering how they were challenging in the top four of the table at all.

The buoyancy of the summer and autumn charge was beginning to sink. Only 17,700 turned up to watch. It might have been cold, and City might have just lost two on the bounce, but there was still a lack of faith outside of the core support that this season was as good as any for years and promised to be a better one once Christmas was over.

City lost 1-0 to Preston. Morrison's absence appeared even more punishing. Even if a centre-half pairing of Manga and Bamba was, in theory, as good as one which included Morrison, the captain's injury was clearly having a mental impact on the team. Maybe people considered City to be a one-man team and that one man was Zohore. After the Preston game, and with Zohore back, the effect of Morrison being missing was leaving more of a mark than if it were any other player.

There was also another obvious lesson from this time, that Lee Tomlin was beginning to look like a spare part, or someone who didn't fit into the side. He was tried as a number 10 to Zohore, a mouthwatering prospect for fans before the season, but it simply didn't work with neither player looking comfortable in the pairing. Their runs and styles of play were out of tune. Tomlin had already had a troubled season, having been charged with, and admitting, affray in an incident at a nightclub in his hometown of Leicester while he was a Bristol City player. That November, he was sentenced and was given 80 hours community service in the area, along with having to pay a small fine. His training with City had to be scheduled around his punishment. Warnock had already been telling the media about Tomlin's fitness problems. His court punishment was not going to help. He might be a talent but that was never likely to make up for his un-Warnock like work rate.

Tomlin wasn't the manager's only problem emerging from Christmas. With Aron Gunnarsson still out, City's midfielders were tiring. Joe Ralls was being burdened with seniority, while Loïc Damour was struggling after being asked to play many more games in his first season of the demanding English Football League than he would have expected. The lack of Morrison magnified this weakness which could only be addressed once the transfer window opened in January.

The fourth game in 10 days, on New Year's Day, was at QPR. Matt Connolly was in the side with Joe Bennett another on the injured list and it couldn't have contrasted more with August's easy romp over the 'Rs'. The Bluebirds were beaten 2-1. Warnock described the defending for the first goal as "Sunday league" standard. Ralls scored a penalty, but it wasn't much consolation.

It had been a dreadful Christmas for Cardiff City, and four defeats in a row highlighted flaws in the squad. Hard work and motivation had pushed the side on from the powerful start in August, but the injuries and the loss of the leader and defensive powerhouse which coincided with that 10 days saw all that begin to unravel.

Would Cardiff have won, or at least not lost, those four Christmas games with Morrison in the side? Who knows? What's certain, though, is that City would have been much better placed to give themselves a chance if he was in the side. Bamba, prone to the odd mistake (a misplaced pass, or over-complication in play) needed Morrison's organising and cajoling. Neil Etheridge looked a better keeper with him in the side, too. The midfield was exposed and Zohore missed Morrison's more accurate cross-field passes and long throws into the penalty box.

City's third round FA Cup tie against Mansfield Town should have been a morale-boosting respite. But City couldn't even beat lower league opposition. At least, though, they didn't concede, drawing 0-0 at home to the Stags. The pleasing news was that Morrison was back, given 75 minutes, and Bennett too was given a game. If nothing else it was a chance for some regrouping before the next round of league matches.

Warnock acknowledges it was a ropey Christmas for his side, you can't argue with that after losing four, but he, and others in that dressing room, would tell you that it was needed to push the players on. The thing that makes this Cardiff City team such a great one – character – is why this period was crucial. Even more so than the extraordinary run that was to follow.

"Morale has never dipped and that's to do with the strength of characters in the dressing room." said Morrison to *WalesOnline*, "People who will bring the mood back up when it's down. I'd like to think I'm one of those! Even when I was sitting in the stands as we were losing games and decisions were going against us, we were never panicking or worrying 'is this our season done?'. Every team in this league goes through a spell like that and, yes, we had a bad 10 or 11 days around Christmas which isn't ideal, but in hindsight that might have kicked us on to not let that happen again. That little blip might actually be the difference between us getting promotion and not."

It sounds counterintuitive doesn't it? How can losses actually be the thing that a team needs? How could those festive defeats have been the difference between the play-offs and going up automatically? Football managers often talk about 'learning lessons' and that's usually a trite response given to a journalist after a loss or mistake. Beyond the cliché, though, this team really did learn something from losing those games. They understood that hard work was the greatest asset they had, that if someone important dropped out – and it would happen again in the season's final months – another would have to step in. It taught them that points are not easily acquired, but are won through commitment and desire. Easy platitudes, but true when it comes to Cardiff's post-Christmas reflections.

Warnock tells me that run armed his side with spirit, gave others confidence and ensured everyone in the squad knew they were valued and valuable. "We lost four games on the trot," he says. "But we regrouped and some of the lads who came in did ever so well and we took off again."

The end of December was the start of something exciting. Warnock could also assess the transfer market to bolster the weaknesses most exposed by the run. Crucially, City were now out of the top two, but it had created a balance in the pack of clubs looking towards the second automatic place. Derby County were now second and City were in third, but remarkably hadn't lost masses of ground on the teams around them and were still only 11 points behind Wolves with plenty of games to come.

Among the players there'd also been winners and losers. City's midfield, without Gunnarsson, needed new bodies and a steadying influence. There was too much for Ralls to handle alone, with Bryson suffering injuries and Damour acclimatising to the British game. Bamba could have been moved into the centre, but that ploy could only ever be a limited success and he could never have been given a go in the centre of the park while Morrison was out as well.

Zohore needed help up front and it was now obvious that Omar Bogle was not meeting Warnock's exacting standards. His sending-off at Bristol City had already marked his card and Warnock hinted at something else, too. Tomlin, meanwhile, just wasn't suited to this team – no matter what Warnock tried. He still looked as though he needed to work on his fitness, and his influence on games wasn't consistent enough to counter the flaws he carried.

In defence, it was now also obvious that Morrison was enormously important. Matt Connolly's return to the first team was welcome for those who remembered him as one of the steadiest players of the Mackay-Solskjaer-Slade eras, and Warnock spoke loyally about him when queries came his way during press conferences, but his multiple injuries had affected the defender and critics of the player sensed his weakness as a full-back against faster opposition. In the centre of defence, Bamba and Manga have the assets which should have made them impregnable, but they could only do so much with a weary midfield in front of them and full-backs pulling them out of position.

Other questions were being asked. Was Neil Etheridge up to the task as keeper? Was too much being asked of Junior Hoilett? Had Nathaniel Mendez-Laing run out of steam already? Could Joe Ralls keep going for the rest of the season? When was Aron Gunnarsson going to be fit again? And when would City start winning again?

January would give answers. The good times weren't far away.

8

Money Talks

"It was the biggest ever achievement because of the circumstances when we arrived. The run Fulham went on, the money other teams spent – Aston Villa, Wolves – Middlesbrough's wage bill was bigger than mine will be in the Premiership!"

Neil Warnock

"What did you think of the Gary Madine signing?" It's a question all City fans have asked themselves after the player was brought in from Bolton Wanderers for £6m. He was a January transfer window target, added much-needed new legs to aid Kenneth Zohore, and put some pressure on his place.

His performances since he joined had hardly lived up to his price tag though, and a scour through Bolton messageboards tells you what they think of how much Warnock paid. Sure, he was a good attacker at Wanderers – but Cardiff had seen no repeat performances. In short, Madine seemed a dud signing.

WalesOnline's Dom Booth was chatting to me about the wonderful 10 months Cardiff City had just enjoyed, and Madine comes up. "The only time I've seen Warnock on the defensive about a player is with Gary Madine," he tells me. Strange because Warnock usually sets the agenda during press conferences. A bit like a politician, he'll give the answers to the questions he thinks should be asked. He'll take the conversation in the direction he wants it to go. "When it came to Gary Madine, money had been spent and Warnock was on the back foot."

His lack of goals, and some glaring misses were scrutinised closely because of the fee. Warnock had spent more on one player than he had on his other 20-odd first team signings in his time at Cardiff. Of course there was more pressure on Madine to succeed than all the others. He was a statement.

Like Lee Tomlin six months earlier, this was a transfer that would be talked about, getting a forward in for big money is always going to enliven the excitement levels. Recruiting Tomlin was all about adding a new creative dimension to City's options, Madine was about adding firepower and competition up front with Danny Ward now out for the rest of the season. It was uncharacteristic for Warnock to spend so much, but nobody could argue that a striker was needed, and in the limited market of January he seemed a sound, if expensive, option.

The reception to his signing proved just how much things had changed among supporters. Instead of applauding the ambition of spending lots on a forward, the question was, could we afford it? 'Cardiff must be mugs to pay that amount for him,' wrote one fan on the *Boltonnuts* website. Another noted: 'In the grand scheme of things, £6m for Madine is a lot of money, much more than he's actually worth. This season he's been banging a few in so far, but I don't expect it to continue, so take advantage whilst he's worth that much.'

It was clear he'd had a good season, and Warnock was drawn to him because, in a team playing Cardiff's kind of football, he was a target for balls knocked long. Warnock also liked his physical presence, as he noted in matches where he started Madine ahead of Zohore. He talked him up where he could, giving him credit for others' successes. He also lauded his impact on Zohore, the Dane did improve after he joined, but would he have hit form anyway? Madine's signing didn't feel like a Warnock thing to do.

Remember, the first thing he'd done when he joined as manager was bring in Sol Bamba and Junior Hoilett, along with Marouane Chamakh – who'd played with Warnock when he was at Crystal Palace – and former England full-back Kieran Richardson. None of them cost a penny in transfer fees and all were willing to join a Championship club in a sticky position. Two of them were arguably amongst the most successful transfers that City have ever made, the other two fading stars whose brief time with the club refreshed the squad, if nothing else.

It could be said that a 50-50 success rate with transfers was about right for Warnock's record in the market. For every fine player, there's been one who didn't quite fit. The brilliance of Warnock's first season at Cardiff, though, was that he brought in so few, so cheaply and was able to turn the side into one showing promotion form. Had he joined even a month earlier, City would probably have found themselves in the play-offs by the end of the season.

Warnock's always been a master in the transfer market. He knows that when he goes into a club, he'll need to spring clean the dressing room. Those who join must have the qualities that Warnock wants, with a willingness to work as important, if not more, than ability. It's why the signings of Lee Tomlin and Gary Madine seem so out of step with the others.

Warnock likes telling the story of how he got Bamba and Hoilett, by making them promise they'd join him wherever he ended up after Rotherham. He'd liked what he'd seen when Bamba faced him as a Leicester player and had tried to sign him at other clubs, but the stars never quite aligned. So when Leeds let Bamba go, the Yorkshireman texted the Ivorian to tell him to sit patiently, he was going to get a club soon and they could finally team up.

Taking up the story, speaking to the *Blakey's Bootroom* podcast, Bamba says: "I missed playing under Neil a few times earlier in my career when I was at Leicester, and when I came back from Palermo and moved to Leeds. He wanted to sign me both times but the circumstances weren't quite perfect. When I left Leeds he said 'just wait, I'm going to get a club'. I knew I would wait because I trust him ... the wages weren't coming in, but we were regularly in contact so I wasn't worried. I waited and I'm now enjoying my best season. I absolutely love the man. I cannot speak highly enough of him."

Hoilett, meanwhile, was also out of work. He'd found himself languishing in the youth team at QPR, cast out of the first team squad, when Warnock took over as caretaker manager there in late 2015. Warnock rescued his Rangers career, putting him back in the starting XI and making him a key part of his team at Loftus Road. "When I walked back in there, he was training with the under-18s as punishment," Warnock recalled a year after bringing Hoilett to Cardiff. "I can't remember why he'd been disciplined – maybe he'd refused a transfer or something – but I said to them when I went in, 'Can I pick anyone who's at the club' and they said yes so I went to see Junior.

"When I spoke to him, I told him I'd tried to sign him two or three times, that he'd be playing that Saturday and that was it. He was amazed. He hadn't played for weeks but I think he was man of the match and since then he's been great for me. He's underrated, one of those that is a first name on the team sheet."

Chamakh and Richardson left in January 2017, with Warnock only moving to sign another player he knew well, Greg Halford from Rotherham, and keeper Allan McGregor on loan from Hull City. He was plotting the following season's manoeuvres. He also knew there was little point getting involved in January's inflated bidding when Cardiff were already looking set for mid-table. Halford was a useful addition to a squad in need of flexibility. He could play in defence or midfield and Warnock appreciated his dressing room qualities along with his adaptability.

A statement was also made that January about Warnock's view of the club's under-23s team. There were too many players in that squad who'd not cracked the first team yet, but who were still on the books despite not looking close to it. This clearly wasn't good for their careers, but it wasn't good for the development of other young players and it wasn't benefitting the first team either.

Warnock let go of players who'd once been tipped to be the next Joe Ledley or Chris Gunter, if not the next Aaron Ramsey, but who'd not lived up to the hype. Even Merthyr-born full-back Declan John, who'd promised so much, was out by the end of 2016-2017. Cardiff's youth academy hadn't produced in years. Joe Ralls, nabbed from Farnborough as a youth player, couldn't be considered a locally-grown talent but he was the nearest City had, and still have, to one who's really made it.

David Tutonda, Tom James, Tommy O'Sullivan and Eli Phillips were released. Of them all, it was James and O'Sullivan who'd looked most likely to make it. James had made an end-of-season appearance in the Premier League and O'Sullivan had once been named Welsh Young Player of the Year. By now, they were in their early 20s, yet the under-23s system (adopted in English football after another reform to youth football) meant they'd hit a ceiling.

In December 2016, and in a prelude to those players' departures, Kevin Nicholson, City's development team manager, left the club and Craig Bellamy was appointed player development manager. It was an ambitious move and one which suited Bellamy, in his education as a coach, and City, in its need to establish more success in its youth system.

"I know that Neil [Warnock] feels Craig's influence here can create greater synergy between our youth players and the first-team, with the ultimate goal of bringing players through to senior football," said chief executive Ken Choo on Bellamy's appointment. "Craig's experience and knowledge of the game speaks for itself and we felt he was the only candidate we wanted to take this critical new position."

"With his experience at the top level, it seemed a shame not to pick his brain. So when the opportunity came, I suggested to Ken Choo that we took him on board," said Warnock at the time. Another club legend, Andy Legg, was appointed to coach the under-23 team. Two revered former players were now in charge of trying to bridge the gap between youth system and first team.

Warnock was happy to fiddle, fix and then give others the responsibility. His ultimate responsibility is to the first team. Making it work makes everything else tick, as Booth explains: "Warnock's not that bothered about the under-23s *per se*, but he is concerned about the people working in the offices and the cleaning lady, making them feel good and bringing them on to the same page. I don't know when it's going to be more productive. In an ideal world he would love it to be, maybe for someone else – Craig Bellamy being the most obvious candidate. I don't think it's come into his thinking a huge amount in the last season because he's been wanting promotion. If you've got a successful first team then it'll follow on from there."

Getting rid of the 22-year-olds going nowhere in the reserves sent a message to younger players in the academy that they'd now get their chance, but it wouldn't last forever. "He has at least changed the way that academy team thinks and that could do something in the future," Booth tells me. He argues that

Warnock's priority, to get Cardiff promoted, means he doesn't have to give much thought to the academy – unless there's a player there who'll do something for the first team. "He doesn't mind giving youngsters a chance and given the right attitude, he'd give them a chance," says Booth. "He did give Mark Harris a go at the end of last season."

The confidence to delegate is another trademark of Warnock's leadership. In the same way that he let Legg and Bellamy get on with the youth teams, so he allowed Ronnie Jepson and Kevin Blackwell, his coaching sidekicks, to do the nitty-gritty stuff on the training field and the tactics board. With that structure in place, Warnock was able to concentrate on wheeling and dealing, once the 2016-17 season had ended.

Releasing players such as Adam Le Fondre and Tom Adeyemi were the less controversial acts of the summer, but the letting go of Peter Whittingham, however, felt brutal. Players of Whittingham's type never fully win over Cardiff fans, but by his final season there was at last an appreciation of his skill and the amazing contribution he'd made in goals and assists in his time as a Bluebird.

Acknowledging his best was now past him was Warnock's bravest and most honest move. Fears that his free kicks, corners, penalties and deft touches would be missed when he was gone were countered as soon as the new season started. "People thought Whittingham would be a bigger loss than he was," says Booth, outlining just how big a statement it was for the City manager. "It was one of the biggest calls Neil Warnock has made at Cardiff, but Whittingham just wasn't a Neil Warnock player. His leaving was a chance for others to come in and take the responsibility."

The signings of Bamba and Hoilett – cheap in cost but priceless in impact – set the benchmark for Warnock's transfer standards. Any player brought in for money would be measured against those two gems. Transfers would be fundamental to progress in 2017-18, and by that summer Warnock must have been desperate for the season to end and the window to open.

He didn't have much money, and he's keen to point out why that makes the promotion that followed so memorable an accomplishment. I asked how proud he was of that season. His answer was pure Warnock: full of pride and emotion, while never forgetting to remind us of the obstacles he'd had to hurl out of his way.

"It was the biggest ever achievement because of the circumstances when we arrived," he says. He had a mess to clear up, but he was also expected to lead whatever was left to at least a play-off place. "The run Fulham went on, the money other teams spent – Aston Villa, Wolves – Middlesbrough's wage bill was bigger than mine will be in the Premiership!"

Warnock may complain, but he knows how good he is at bargain hunting. The rule of thumb: the less spent on a player, the more successful a signing; followed that summer. Nathaniel Mendez-Laing, Neil Etheridge and Callum Paterson came cheap. Few knew anything about them. Yet, they, along with Bamba and Hoilett, were consistently first team first choices and among the best performers in the division, whatever the end-of-season team-of-the-years said.

"My player of the season has to be Bamba," says Sarah McCreadie. "He's the heartbeat of the team and has personified us as a side this season, with his all his power, skill and never-say-die attitude. He's an incredible leader, who is just as likely to take your breath away in wonder with some audacious skill as he is a spectacular tackle. He's become my favourite Cardiff player ever."

Etheridge, though, was one of Warnock's most outstanding purchases. Picked up from Walsall, out of contract, he looked certain to be back-up to Lee Camp – another free transfer during pre-season – but Camp was hit by injuries and never found himself near the first team. Philippines international Etheridge had, in the years leading up to his City career, found himself sleeping on friends' sofas as he was loaned out and released by lower league clubs before almost leaving the game altogether when it looked like no club wanted him.

"I was an academy player, I went from Chelsea to Fulham, two Premier League teams at the time, and I was sitting on the bench in the Europa League and the Premier League. You don't think it's going to finish, but that's part of being a footballer," he told *WalesOnline*.

He sold his house and cars and was close to returning to the Philippines. "It's a tough industry to be in. I can look back at it now and it's made me a much stronger person. I got offered a contract from Oldham to sit on the bench, and I did it. I was living on my mate's sofa, but that's what you've got to do to get by."

His confidence may have taken a while to build, but by the second half of the season, he had a flourishing Championship career. Etheridge played in all but one league game, keeping 19 clean sheets and letting only 37 goals past him. He was an integral part of the defence and arguably the most improved player from the beginning to the end of the season.

Warnock did spend money during the summer transfer window, on Danny Ward, Lee Tomlin and Omar Bogle. Three forwards, all different types of player, none a resounding success. Ward's season finished just as it looked as though he was the player to complement and compete with Kenneth Zohore. Alas it wasn't to be. Ward scored four goals in 20 appearances, many from the bench, before ending his season with injury in December's home match against Norwich.

Bogle was brought in for £700,000 from Wigan in August, a transfer nobody saw coming. He scored goals, had plenty of running in him, was direct and enthusiastic. Then came the red card at Bristol City, and a defeat which almost certainly would've been avoided without it. Warnock was furious. By January he was out on loan to Peterborough. Don't ever get on the wrong side of Neil Warnock. "I think he's got to go and play," Warnock explained after the January window closed, hinting at other issues. "The red card was a disappointment to me but other things as well. It's an opportunity for him to go in the shop window and get some goals now."

If Ward was full of promise and Bogle was a surprise and then a let-down, then Lee Tomlin was the ultimate footballing anticlimax. It would be cruel to call him a flop, but he wasn't far off it, considering his reputation and the fact he was nabbed from rivals Bristol City. Talk that the transfer cost Cardiff near £3m was dismissed by Warnock, who also took issue with comments made by Peterborough chairman Darragh MacAnthony that the player was earning £28,000 a week when he told his fans he'd wanted to sign Tomlin that summer too. "We only paid £1.5m," said an angry Warnock in response. "I think everybody knows that, and not £2.9m – and I bet Tomlin wishes he was on that sort of money. He's nowhere near that, miles away."

By January, Tomlin had made only 13 appearances – most either coming off the bench or being substituted himself – and had scored just one goal. Hanging over the player's head was the court case in Leicester, which Warnock admitted had affected Tomlin. There was also the matter of fitness. When talking about the player, Warnock remained an admirer of his ability. "Lee knows he's a matchwinner for us, but we've got to try and hope he can eventually start a game rather than just be a substitute," he told reporters. "He has to work very hard at his fitness which he doesn't find easy. Some people are naturally fit. It's not all about doing the wrong things because he is working very hard and we need him to because we've got to have people who can change and win matches for us in the second half of the season."

He eventually lost patience. Tomlin didn't meet Warnock's needs for the second half of the season, with City locked in a battle for automatic promotion with four or five other clubs. The player was loaned out to Nottingham Forest, where he teamed up with his old Middlesbrough boss Aitor Karanka. Everything had been tried, Warnock said, to get Tomlin up to the fitness standards he demanded but nothing worked. He couldn't do with having the player around for such a critical period, so opted to take Forest's Jamie Ward on loan in return. Two more contrasting players there could not be, but Warnock said he was a fan of Ward's flexibility, work rate and his gift – so he said – for finding the net.

Tomlin's City career ended before it had begun, argues Booth. "The success of the 4-3-3 formation with hard-working players throughout that, meant Lee Tomlin couldn't really fit in," he says. Booth points to just how different Tomlin's treatment was to the others in the squad, maybe because so much money had been spent and so much expectation had been placed on him.

It might have been that he'd taken a look at Tomlin in training and didn't fancy him because of that.

"No matter how hard he tried and failed, he was given as much chance as possible, he was given special measures in training." It didn't work. Excited fans wanted it to, desperately. He was the "bit of luxury", Booth says, they desired in the team. "The games Tomlin played, he was a class act, I thought. Even in the games where you thought Warnock could afford to play him, he didn't.

"A hardworking trio and three quick forward players had worked so well early on in the season, Tomlin was just a bad fit. I think Warnock just grew tired of it, but with Tomlin and Bogle there were clearly issues behind the scenes that had angered him, but I think he managed both situations well, right up to the end."

The relative failure of Tomlin and Bogle and to a much lesser extent, Ward (without his injury his story would've been completely different) mattered little considering Warnock's broader transfer successes. Bamba, Hoilett, Etheridge, Mendez-Laing, Paterson, Loïc Damour were all hits. All permanent signings and only Paterson costing anything in terms of an upfront fee.

Then there was Warnock's use of the loan market. He bolstered squad numbers with Craig Bryson from Derby, a midfielder Warnock spoke highly of; Liam Feeney, a winger from Blackburn; and in January came young Serbian international Marko Grujić from Liverpool to strengthen the midfield and bring some quality to the centre of the park. He's one better suited to the more forgiving Premier League than the non-stop Championship, but he still managed to add something which had been lacking. Jamie Ward, Yanic Wildschut and Armand Traoré came in on loan too, only to play the smallest of bit-part roles during their stay.

Bryson may have frustrated supporters (he'd often seem to run into space only for the ball to land in the spot where he'd come from, or do the same with a pass to a teammate) but Warnock celebrated the Scotland international's work rate and busy demeanour, knowing what fans were saying about the player. He did the same with Feeney, another who left some feeling bemused, but who Warnock praised as a seasoned Championship player.

Then there was Madine, who cost a fortune but scored none and missed many in his 13 City appearances. If you believe Warnock's claim it pushed Zohore to his best – it was £6m well spent.

Warnock was consistent – and maybe defensive – about Madine's performances and impact, saying he was going to pair him and Zohore together (though never did, always opting for a lone front man instead), and that he should have signed the former Bolton player months earlier, such was his impact on his teammate. "We would not be anywhere near where we are now if he had not signed," Warnock told BBC Wales in April and claimed he'd never been happier with a signing in his career.

Warnock had tinkered in all the right places in a very short time to make that possible but the peculiarity of Madine and Tomlin prove how difficult it is to get a transfer right every time. That he'd made so many in less than a year, most of whom were a success, demonstrates Warnock's skill at doing deals and finding new talent. He'd lived up to his reputation and then some, bringing in 20 first-teamers on loan, and permanently, and shipping dozens out. The quality of the squad was raised, but the complexion of its personality was different too. It was more robust, more together, more ready to deal with mistakes and upsets. This reliance would be its great strength after the four games of Christmas.

9

New Year Blues

"Neil Warnock created the atmosphere in the club that it probably hasn't had since Eddie May – everyone was in it together and everyone supports the club because of the manager. He engaged with the fans. People feel he is a proper football manager."

Phil Nifield

The seeds of Cardiff's promotion were planted in August, and Christmas was its blossoming. Those matches in the first months of 2018 were the ripening fruits in the club's race to the Premier League.

City had decided the season was back on. Defeat at QPR was the last of the very worst. "This team has so much heart in it," explains fan James Leighton. "All of us knew through our history that Cardiff have had a tendency to blow it and bottle it when it's come to the crucial games, throughout the club's entire history really. With Neil Warnock I sensed that he would not allow that to happen."

Many thought otherwise. The carnage of late December was a reality check. Cardiff City weren't up to it, the promotion dream was over, it'd be hard work to go up – maybe impossible. The play-offs it would have to be, or nothing. Cardiff supporters can be forgiven for being pessimistic. Rather than criticise it, it's better to understand it. For generations, teams have teetered on the brink of brilliance, only for everything to come crashing down.

From Jimmy Scoular's perennial almost-rans of the 1960s and early 1970s, when the sale of John Toshack undermined any hope of getting to the top flight for generations to come, dark histories have fuelled the mythology of Cardiff City. There was the despair of the 1980s, the what-could-have-beens of the 1990s, the if-onlys of the Sam Hammam years. Hopes have been dashed and dreams have been broken.

Cardiff have managed to mangle their opportunities. It's what makes being a City fan all at once so great and yet, so painful. True or not, for this is a club which hasn't been relegated from Championship level since it arrived back in 2003, the myth has stuck. You're not a real City fan unless you expect to feel the crushing pain of despair over the unalloyed rapture of celebration.

No doubt, Leighton was in a minority. When it came to the end of season speeches, Warnock made plain he knew that as well. After being held to a 0-0 draw by Macclesfield Town at home, with just 6,378 watching, City faced Sunderland. The game had plenty of interesting little narratives within it: the return of Chris Coleman to his old Wales fortress; Sunderland's catastrophic decline; and Cardiff's stuttering promotion hopes. Any doubts about City's capabilities were brushed aside in that game, after the visitors were beaten 4-0. It was watched on TV by one Marko Grujić, and it was apparently enough to persuade him to join the Bluebirds.

Confidence was low though, admitted Warnock afterwards. Four losses over Christmas hit morale. Those words which had become absolutely crucial to the season's momentum so far, 'hard work', were so important now, because a team low on

109

confidence needs to work hard to regain it. City ground out the first goal or two, before easing past Coleman's struggling side as their self-belief grew.

Maybe it helped that Cardiff's losing streak came in the blink of an eye – four losses over just 10 days. Recovering from this nightmare at Christmas was easier, the mental scar quicker to heal.

Strange that in this season City were on the brink of their worst league run in two decades. That they came back from it exemplifies how good they actually were.

Sunderland marked the beginning of an unbeaten run that would go on well into spring, including a run of wins which put this side on the brink of matching another club record. A goalless draw at Sheffield Wednesday was followed by a resounding 4-1 win over Leeds United at Elland Road. Another big statement and second place wasn't looking so far away.

Warnock was keen to stress the second half of the season would be about enjoyment, no pressure.

Afterwards, he told the *Yorkshire Post*: "We've improved the squad in the window with players coming in – and it was pleasing to see Gary Madine make his debut, but we've also got players to come back as well, like Gunnarsson. So, let's enjoy the second half of the season." It was more deliberate language at work.

Next up, another game live on Sky, as City travelled to Millwall – similar overachievers, that season the Lions were in with an unlikely shot at the play-offs. It had been a scrappy game, and one that Cardiff arguably deserved to win. A sense of injustice was reinforced when the referee blew his whistle for a foul on Joe Bennett, having let play continue, just as Sol Bamba shot and scored what should have been the winning goal in the dying moments of injury time. Warnock was incensed.

"I think it's appalling at this level", he said. "Sol is going to shoot and then he blows. I don't accept that. He is a really experienced referee and I feel let down. He cost us the game. We are fighting to get in the Premier League. But for the referee it would have been three points." Another reason to get angry. More emotional fuel to fire the push to the Premier League.

Themes about this side were now emerging, its personality was maturing: Callum Paterson was an attacking threat; the defence was solid – especially with the return of Sean Morrison; the class of Neil Etheridge in goal; the emergence of Joe Ralls as a midfielder of assured quality; the hard-working wing play. More than those things and whatever else you could say, it was the squad's resilience which marked it out. It was about now that City fans really started to fall in love with the side.

"The football itself hasn't been the prettiest you've ever seen but it's very effective," says lifelong fan Philip Nifield. "Compare it to that Dave Jones team which didn't get promoted but often played fantastic football. Warnock used people to their strengths and he's got them playing the way he wants to. He's created a team, which is the most important thing. It's why Aston Villa and Derby didn't go up. He created a real team ethos. Nobody is bigger than the team, even the better players, and they all bought into it."

Speaking to fans about Warnock's side, there's almost always a reference point, or rather person, it returns to: Eddie May. Few managers have managed to connect with City fans in the way May had back in the early 1990s.

Leighton again: "This season has been right up there with the best, but the Eddie May season will always be at the top for me. It was my first real taste of success for Cardiff City and the team had players like Nathan Blake, Kevin Ratcliffe and Robbie James in it. This Neil Warnock team is very similar to that Eddie May one, with its never-say-die attitude. Other promotion seasons we'd gone up as favourites a lot of the time, but this one was a lovely surprise in a way."

Nifield agrees. Results and promotion, of course those have been crucial things, but the season has been as important, he says, for regenerating the ethos and identity of Cardiff City. "In some ways the results were less important because so many people stopped going and weren't interested in Cardiff City, but Warnock created the atmosphere in the club that it probably hasn't had since May – everyone was in it together and everyone supports the club because of the manager. He engaged with the fans. People feel he is a proper football manager."

As City's form in the league returned, there was a small break from the Championship with an FA Cup fixture against Manchester City, a taster of the challenge ahead if promotion was secured. There was to be no repeat of the 1994 FA Cup epic, when Nathan Blake's wonderful winning goal and Mark Grew's penalty save saw the Bluebirds beat a very different incarnation of the Sky Blues 1-0. This time it was 2-0 to a classy Manchester City who rarely looked as though they were going through the gears. The result was irrelevant, really, but there was one rather more interesting talking point to emerge (other than the record attendance for a home game at the new ground, now 32,339).

It came after the sending off of Joe Bennett for a second yellow card. He'd been aggressive through the match and could have gone in the first half for a late tackle on Leroy Sane. The scything down of Brahim Diaz forced ref Lee Mason into action. Bennett was off. Warnock was displeased. "It's unprofessional from Joe and then to commit one in the 92nd minute," he told BBC Wales. "Maybe he doesn't want to go to Leeds on Saturday. He will be training morning, noon and night, I can tell you that."

Bennett became the victim of outrage on social media as Sane had been injured and both of Bennett's victims could've been damaged much more. The left-back might have found himself outcast, like Omar Bogle following his dismissal at Bristol City which had so infuriated Warnock in the autumn, but he wasn't. He was given some punishment, yet he came back stronger and better for that experience. Some of his performances at full-back were as good as any in the position for City in living memory.

Perhaps he had something to prove after the criticism from the football community, maybe it was the shot in the arm he needed to take his career further forward, but Bennett truly arrived as a Cardiff City player when he came back from suspension after the FA Cup debacle.

It was an important moment for him and for the Cardiff promotion story, because in the Neil Warnock set up, full-backs and wingers are among the most valuable players. So much is asked of wide men who must not only set up goal chances and score themselves, but also track back and defend when they're needed. Full-backs, meanwhile, are essential pieces in the defensive machinery. Warnock's public punishment of Bennett, in a way which couldn't really be questioned, was key in the player's renewal. Things were beginning to click again.

After the Millwall game came win after win after win. The Bluebirds looked unstoppable. Bolton, Middlesbrough, Ipswich and Bristol City fell first. Then came the first snow of the late winter freeze and a postponed match at Brentford. Barnsley and Birmingham were next, then Brentford away in the rearranged game with the Bees.

If any performance of the season represented the new Warnock Cardiff City, this was it. Despite City now being back in second place, there was a sense that Brentford posed a massive test. They were an attacking threat, admired by owner Vincent Tan for their prolific number of shots on goal.

City breezed past Brentford with a 3-1 win. They were ruthless, professional, free-scoring, and miserly in defence.

They absorbed Brentford's possession and countered the goal they conceded first with quick, incisive football. It wasn't the *laissez faire* stuff of August and September, it wasn't the miserable football of Christmas – it was hard work, not giving up, and believing in yourself. Warnock was delighted.

"Many teams would have gone under tonight with the start we had and the way they were playing – but boy we hung in there and showed the character we've got," he told *cardiffcityfc.co.uk*. "We've not played against anything like that all season. They got the goal and could have got a couple more – a great save from Neil [Etheridge] kept us in it." He spoke of his pride at the fans, but most of all, of the enormous pride in his players and their spirit. "I look around the dressing room before a game and I think: 'Wow, I'm glad these are my lads.'"

It was now seven wins in a row. The club record was nine. The last time City had come close to equalling or beating that record was in 1992-93 – that Eddie May team again – when they won 10 out of 11 on an unbeaten run which lasted from January to March. Not even Malky Mackay's title-winning side, which romped so easily to promotion, could manage anything like that. The last time City had won six in a row was in 2000-01, when Alan Cork led the Bluebirds to promotion from the Third Division. February and March were an exciting – if exceptionally cold – couple of months.

"This has been my favourite season supporting the club," commented Sarah McCreadie. "Something has finally overtaken the 2008 FA Cup final season. It would still be my favourite even if we hadn't achieved promotion. This is the kind of season and team and manager that you'd wait forever for. I can't compare this promotion season to our last – due to the situation with the rebranding of the club it felt numb to me but this one...oh baby! I loved every second."

City were seven points clear of third place Aston Villa by the time it came to the scheduled fixture against Derby County in March. It proved one of the most controversial moments of the season.

"We've got a couple more on the treatment table, unfortunately," Rams manager Gary Rowett told the *Derby Telegraph* before the game. "We've got 10 senior players training this morning. It's quite a ridiculous scenario. If we had some under-23s on the bench at Forest, we might have some under-16s on the bench this weekend! We're just trying to get through this last game before the international break."

A cynic would say they weren't trying to get through it at all. Derby had dropped to fifth and their winless run of seven contrasted with the buoyant form of the Bluebirds. Warnock was glowing, pre-match about his opponents. "It's a lovely stadium and there'll be a fabulous crowd. I always like going there and enjoyed going to the old Baseball Ground, too. They are good football people (in Derby)."

His views had been shaped by years working in the region. He played for Chesterfield and was manager of Notts County and Burton, where he also played. He knew the area and remembered Derby's famous old ground fondly. That fondness would quickly dry up.

More snow had fallen across Wales and England that mid-March weekend. Despite south Wales being badly been hit, thousands of excited supporters had travelled up early in the morning. To Cardiff's astonishment, the noon game was called off at 9am. The first hint of controversy was a Twitter post by the Derby club shop saying it was still open for business despite the match being postponed. Then Cardiff City fans began arriving at Pride Park and seeing roads and car parks free of snow.

As the day went on, the story moved quickly. Derby's police and council distanced themselves from the decision. Furious

Cardiff fans tweeted about a lack of snow, even City's players posted pictures on Twitter of Pride Park's clear surrounds. Utility player Greg Halford captioned his with a sarcastic: 'Need a plough to get through the snow today for the game. Not surprised it's called off.'

Cardiff submitted a dossier to the English Football League outlining why the match should have gone ahead and Warnock vented his spleen. The match had been scheduled to be shown on Sky Sports, and Warnock told the broadcaster: "I'm sorry, I can't accept that today – it's not safe? We have come out from the middle of the countryside in the coach and the roads have been perfectly all right, so I just don't know where they are coming from with this. It leaves a sour taste for all the people that have travelled.

"I am very disappointed obviously. I am not overly surprised, if I am honest, after I heard Gary [Rowett's] remarks earlier in the week [about their 'injury crisis']. You look at the game two weeks ago against Fulham here, it was 10 times worse. There were snow ploughs outside. As you see here the car parks are clear, all the shops are open."

From Cardiff's perspective you can see why there was anger that a game which was so winnable, which kept that crucial momentum going, had been called off. Warnock's comments did not endear him to an already hostile crowd. Nor did the fact that Derby's decision was vindicated. The EFL found them not at fault in the postponement. Whatever Cardiff's dossier said – there was nothing wrong with the decision so there was no reason to sanction the Rams over it.

When video emerged of Sean Morrison goading Derby players (it was nothing but WhatsApp fun between the two squads, of the sort no doubt played out by professionals around the country, but – when leaked publicly – looked childish and inappropriate without context), there was even more antagonism between the clubs. Warnock said he'd reminded Morrison of his position as captain and his job as a role model. "When you first hear about that, you think 'oh no', but when you see the videos our lads have got – which we're not prepared to release – it's just banter really and a lot of hot air, it just makes it more mouthwatering when we play them in a couple of weeks."

The episode didn't matter massively when it came to City's hopes of getting out of the division, and it was quickly forgotten about, but it provided another slapstick scene in the Derby game pantomime. With the match off (and Cardiff fans' travel expenses reimbursed by Vincent Tan), that crucial flow from the winning run began to melt with the slush around Pride Park. City did beat their next opponents, Burton Albion, at home 3-1 but that was it. The run was about to end.

Eight in a row was an amazing achievement nevertheless. To have come within one win of the club record, held by the fine post-war Bluebirds of 1946-47, would have been unthinkable before the season began. Already this side had achieved a club record for the brilliant start to the campaign, and after Christmas they had done something no City side had done for 25 years.

Some big teams were beaten, too, in that eight-match run. Middlesbrough, with their big budget, and Ipswich, whose season was fizzling out but who'd been a big threat early on in the season. There were the hot shots of Brentford and teams fighting for their Championship survival – Birmingham, Bolton and Burton. Never a simple task in the division to take on such teams and beat them so consistently, such is the nature of the Championship – it's one of the things Warnock famously loves about it: anybody can beat anybody else on their day, no matter what position they're in. To achieve wins so consistently is above anything Cardiff should've been doing. They simply weren't well resourced enough to do something like that.

It's easy to label it a miracle. It really wasn't anything like a supernatural event, but in the cosetted world of football – where there are only finite possibilities and objectives – it was as close to miraculous as you could get. A team comprising mainly free transfers, with a couple from the lower leagues, should not be able to do anything like that in the second tier.

Eight wins in a row is a feat worth celebrating. Fans should be proud their team were able to do it during this season of all seasons, and they should treasure the memories – such runs come round once in a generation, the statistics say so. Only in the realms of fantasy could the Bluebirds do anything like that in the Premier League.

How did it end? In a 1-1 draw at Warnock's footballing home, Bramall Lane. Even at this disappointing moment (the record wasn't equalled and the run was over), the immense determination epitomised the season. In fact, at the end of the game, after being behind for most of it, Anthony Pilkington's injury time equaliser (by now he was a true supersub and playing his most effective football in a City shirt, despite not being in the starting XI), made the draw feel more like a win. A point salvaged from the jaws of defeat. Sheffield United probably deserved to win it, they looked stronger than the weary Cardiff team which fought out that draw, but nobody really cared. All that mattered was points and the Bluebirds were one point closer to living the promotion dream.

Warnock was now entering all-out psychological war with the managers and teams competing with City for second place. Despite the train of victories coming to an end, he was aware that this draw was a win.

He said Wolves, Aston Villa and Fulham would be "gutted" at another Cardiff comeback. "Likewise, I'm sure people like Middlesbrough will be over the moon and people at the top end play-off-wise," he said. "They'll be looking at Sheffield United because they would have gone into the top six, wouldn't they? We're all at it. We're all looking at the top 10 and at the play-offs, and quite rightly so. I just feel it could be the best point of the season that, in the circumstances."

There were now seven games left, and City had already accumulated 80 points, but it wasn't enough to keep the strong chasing pack off the Bluebirds' tails. Fulham were eight points behind Cardiff, and Villa a further two points adrift. Though the games were running out, a drop in form for Cardiff (remember anything's possible in the Championship and that's why we love it), could mean Fulham would beat them to one of the automatic places.

On the other hand, with Wolves still to play City in Cardiff, it was possible the Bluebirds could win that and open up the race for the title once more. Every one of the top four were due a dip. Who would it be and how would they cope?

Cardiff's run-in was tough. It included Villa, Wolves and that rearranged game at Derby. The other four games were winnable, but even teams with nothing to play for in the Championship don't like giving wins away for free. Every point would have to be worked for doubly hard, the runs at the beginning of the season and after Christmas had given Cardiff the advantage, but the final games would be the greatest test of resilience faced yet. Promotion might have been within their sights, but it was far from secure.

"I want excitement. The Sheffield United game was quite exciting even though we didn't play very well," said Warnock, enjoying this end-of-season uncertainty. "We've already had a remarkable season if you look at the odds, and hopefully in the last six games we can prove we're up there on merit, we are getting better. It would be a miracle, the best achievement in my career by a mile."

Always expect the unpredictable. Each year provides drama. Wolves were next up. It would be the greatest test of the season – and there were more to come.

10

Our Time

"I've seen the lads grow up. We get criticised but when you look at our games from a neutral point of view, they're always exciting games and we've pleased our fans. It takes all in the world of football. There's never a dull moment."

Neil Warnock

Vincent Tan, dressed in a blue Cardiff City shirt, is being carried off the pitch like a trophy on the shoulders of a group of misty-eyed fans. In four years he's gone from the most vilified character in the city to everyone's favourite uncle at a drunken family wedding. This 'utterly extraordinary' season (how *The Guardian* saw Cardiff's promotion) just got more surreal.

Things had come a full circle. Now, instead of City fans hating what the club had become, everyone else hated Cardiff. For the most brilliant of reasons. May 6, at roughly 2.25pm, marked the ultimate conclusion in this story, the point the club's red wall was totally knocked down and reduced to dust, almost as if it had never happened. Almost.

Fireworks boomed into the blue firmament above the stadium. Lucky blue. This was meant to be.

It felt fateful after the Reading match that day, but not long before we'd all had the jitters. Six games earlier, things had even got a bit nasty. The in-fighting within the club was over, but the nerves were getting to Warnock – who'd just been named Championship manager of the season, despite promotion a far-from foregone conclusion.

So much was expected from a top-of-the-table clash against Wolves. It had promised drama and certainly delivered, particularly in the final moments of the game when, gallingly, Cardiff missed two injury time penalties, losing 1-0 to the league leaders. The failure to win a point was as dispiriting an end to the game as any since City's Wembley losses to Blackpool in the play-offs, or Liverpool in the League Cup final.

After the final whistle, Wolves' ecstatic manager Nuno Espirito Santo had shown a lack of manners by running past Warnock's outstretched hand, on his way to celebrate with his players and fans. Given the way the game was won and what it meant for his own side's promotion chances, Nuno's emotional *faux pas* was understandable, but his lack of common courtesy and neglect of football's traditional post-match protocol couldn't be excused.

Warnock, snubbed and indignant, showed his anger by refusing to shake Nuno's hand when it was offered a short while later. "Why would I speak to him?" He responded to reporters who told him Nuno wanted to personally apologise for his conduct. "I don't want to. He can say anything after the game. I'm talking about when the whistle goes, what he should do, the etiquette, the manners, the class. They've won the game, for God's sake. He should shake your hand and say 'unlucky'. You don't have to run off like that and rub your nose in it. A disgrace." He had a point.

A loss, but it was a thrilling game against undoubtedly the top team in the division, and another record crowd at the

Cardiff City Stadium. Warnock had described the season as "one hell of a roller coaster" and it wasn't his time to get off yet.

The Wolves match was peculiar. It had the hallmarks of a classic Cardiff City performance: ceding possession, but having more shots on goal, and winning the corners count. Yet it was also lacking a late point-saving, or win-securing, goal – thanks to a goalie's save and a cross bar which got in the way of the two late penalties.

Other teams would have crumbled after that heartbreak and fans wondered if City had blown their chance again. This feeling of impending doom increased after the defeat against Aston Villa four days later. It was the first time since February that the Bluebirds had dropped out of the top two.

This team had fight, though, and fan James Leighton needed to kick himself to remember that. "I remember after the Wolves game feeling like it was the end of the world," he says. "But as the days went on, I reminded myself how this team has scored so many last-minute goals – they just grind things out, they couldn't and wouldn't slip up.

"We went to Norwich and scored two late goals and it was proof that this team was gutsy. Any time any club got ahead of us, whether it was Derby, Aston Villa or Fulham, they were only there for a week or two before they bottled it. Every time Fulham were there, they choked. We fought back again and again."

The two late goals at Norwich pushed City back up to second place and tightened the chase for automatic promotion. The pressure was back on Fulham. City made things more fraught for the Cottagers by beating Nottingham Forest the week after, before travelling back up to Derby for the rearranged game with the Rams. There was no chance of snow cancelling this one, with the spring thaw finally underway, and some travelling City fans dressed up as snowmen in a pointed dig at the hosts.

The 3-1 defeat was disappointing and the performance underwhelming. A glaring Gary Madine miss was frustrating. There were also worrying signs of some uncharacteristic defensive frailties. The verbal sparring over the cancelled match was finished as far as Warnock was concerned. "I'm definitely not going to give you any extra lines that you want," he'd told the pre-match press conference. "I've listened to some presenters asking questions to managers at difficult times and I cringe. We're just looking forward to the three games, not just Derby. They're a proper football club, and one I wish I could've managed in the past. They've always got a really loud backing and there's a lot of pressure on them to get into the play-offs. It's set up to be a cracking game."

The Derby loss hurt Warnock as deeply as any before. Sharon even travelled up to Wales afterwards to be at his side. The reality was that by this stage of the season, City couldn't dwell for long on let-downs. Yes the Derby result was disappointing, but rueing missed chances and bemoaning defensive errors wasn't going to win back those lost points. The following Saturday, Cardiff had another trip north to Hull, who'd underachieved, having been relegated from the Premier League the year before. With the Derby defeat forgotten, Cardiff breezed past the Tigers with a 2-0 win, both goals coming from Sean Morrison – his transformation into City's Captain Marvel (as Tan called him at the end of season awards) now complete.

Morrison had scored some crucial goals throughout the season. His second at Hull wasn't a usual set-piece header, it came after a counter-attack by Nathaniel Mendez-Laing who'd run almost the full length of the pitch with the ball. The captain, oddly, had run with him and was ready and waiting for the pass into the penalty area, controlling the ball and taking on defenders like an in-form striker.

Wolves had now secured promotion, as champions, and the fight for second, with Villa having fallen away, was now between City and Fulham. Wily old Warnock was doing his very best to protect his squad and put the pressure back on the Cottagers. It set things up very nicely for the last game – a home match against Reading – with City just needing to win or equal whatever Fulham did at Birmingham.

"I felt sick watching that final game against Reading," says Sarah McCreadie. "I couldn't enjoy it until the final whistle." Even Warnock admitted he was nervous. "I've always had nerves, since I was at Gainsborough," he told the pre-match press conference, referring to his first job in management. "It's just the opportunity to get that eighth promotion and I didn't think it could come this quick. I've seen the lads grow up, we get criticised but when you look at our games from a neutral point of view, they're always exciting games and we've pleased our fans. It takes all sorts in the world of football. There's never a dull moment."

The manager urged supporters to enjoy the moment. He told reporters: "All season it's been great – I look at the forums – and when you go back to August, I wish I could talk to some of those guys now. As the season has progressed, it's been interesting to see the fans' reactions, but the biggest plus for me is that I've managed to bring the whole club together over 18 months. It was very fragmented but now, from the owner Vincent to the cleaning girls, we're all in it together and the boys have shown that on the pitch. It's a great team spirit which has got us where we are."

Warnock was confident of getting City up, whatever the scenario. His track record in the so-called lottery of the play-offs – "I'm quite good at them, me" – is excellent. Among those eight promotions are a fair few Wembley wins (four play-off final victories in all) so if the worst case scenario happened, it wasn't the end of the road for the Bluebirds' odyssey back to the Premier League.

Warnock had carefully pieced together the fragments of a priceless football family, whose scattered shards had been broken into thousands of tiny pieces, like a skilled conservator rebuilding a smashed Ming vase. He'd not been merely preserving a beloved artefact, he'd discovered new value, and the final part of the process hinged on this Reading game. It had come down to the last match – we knew that it would. All of Cardiff had come out to party, just in case. Police closed Cowbridge Road East as fans took over the road – Salvatore Vara, co-owner of Calabrisella, watched it all from the top floor window.

The popular Italian restaurant is bang in the middle of a pre-match drinking quadrant of pubs, which now looked and sounded like a carnival. "It was amazing to see everybody so happy, crowds carrying a huge Cardiff City flag that took up the whole street," says the Reggina (and Cardiff) fan. "We sold a lot of pizza and a lot of beer!" Salvatore's video of the scene, uploaded live to Facebook, was watched over 20,000 times. "The party atmosphere carried on all day and night," he said. "Loads of our customers are City fans and it's been brilliant to see them so excited."

What a contrast to the sheepish way Cardiff 'celebrated' the last promotion. This was a day for everyone, whatever they thought of what had happened before, to unite and have the time of their lives being a Bluebird. Hours before the midday kick off, Jubilee Park (the old football pitch in the shadow of the Cardiff City Stadium, used as a training ground by hard-up squads of City past) was packed with chanting crowds. People brought their babies. The whole city showed up.

Being a Cardiff City fan hasn't always been an easy thing to admit. All the way from the 1980s' chronic hooliganism to not that long ago, when every other team either felt sorry for us ("are you back to Blue yet"?) or was laughing in our faces. Now, it was cool to be a Bluebird again. That afternoon, the volume at the stadium was turned to the maximum. Tense? You'd better believe it. But that didn't stop the crowd making one hell of a noise.

Warnock's programme notes for that game read like a manager who knew his team were going up. 'We've probably surprised a few of our supporters by how far we've come within a short time,' he wrote, showing his obvious pride at managing Cardiff City like he was describing his firstborn, 'but we have a really good group at the moment and they never cease to amaze me on a daily basis. These last few weeks, I've never known a squad with such togetherness. Even the lads who haven't been in the matchday 18 have been a joy to work with.'

The scenes and sounds in the stadium were unbelievable and the excitement was palpable as the fans sensed something special was about to happen. Yet, as McCreadie says: "Even when everyone was cheering around me as the goals from the Fulham game were coming through to us, I still wouldn't let myself believe it. I was still thinking that somehow Fulham would come back."

With pockets of phone-watchers keeping one eye on the other game, the flow of news got chaotic. Spontaneous cheers would erupt as Fulham struggled at St Andrews. Someone would shout that Fulham had gone ahead. Cheers would spread like a Mexican wave, the news of the latest from the Midlands eventually rippling through the stands. Cardiff, in the middle of all of this, had left their scoring boots behind, never taking any of their chances, but it didn't matter. Birmingham were doing the job for City, walloping Fulham 3-1.

By the third Birmingham goal, in the 89th minute, panicked City coach Kevin Blackwell was running over to the Canton End to urge fans to get back to their seats after a pre-emptive pitch invasion saw supporters spill onto the grass when they thought it was all over.

Like others around the stadium, Clive Rees – a fan of 40 years – was keeping up on the Fulham latest via shouts from his neighbours in the stands. "The game itself was a bit flatish," he said. "As soon as it became clear Reading had come with a game-plan, that they were sticking to, you felt City weren't going to score, but the news from Birmingham was lifting us and keeping the atmosphere going."

As the third official held up his board showing five minutes of injury time, Reading's place in the Championship was secured, and Cardiff City were in the Premier League.

The Royals' two centre-halves passed the ball between them, City's Gary Madine directing them not to play it forward as the game petered out, before the ref called an end to it all, putting us all out of our misery.

"When the whistle blew I was so, so happy," says McCreadie. "We'd done it. After all the team's hard work and after being up the top all season, I felt we really deserved it. It felt completely different from the last time we went up. I felt like I'd waited all my life for this one. I was right up the top of the stadium but there was no way I was missing out on getting on that pitch – I told my mum 'We're going!' and we climbed over countless seats to get there. It felt like a dream being on the pitch, where I'd watched this wonderful season play out, and looking around at everyone so happy around me. I stole a bit of grass, too."

With the match over, fans clambered over the advertising hoardings and ran towards the dugout for the pitch invasion proper to start. No player in a blue shirt could get to the tunnel without being smothered. Lee Peltier crowd-surfed his way over the delirious fans. When the team finally made it through the ring of stewards holding back more and more fans, they were given a hug, handshake and a word in their ear one-by-one by an ecstatic Warnock, waiting for them before they reached the dressing room.

Eventually, the squad made it to the directors' box, an elevated position so everyone in the ground could see them, and Morrison lifted the promotion trophy. They were joined by Tan and his entourage but it was clear the owner was sharing in the partying rather than taking it over. This was as egalitarian as celebrations get. They chanted his name and sang "We'll Always Be Blue." Tan smiled and cheered, did a few Ayatollahs, and showed off his blue City top.

Warnock later thanked fans with the ultimate tribute – in more than 50 years in football, he'd not experienced an atmosphere like this one. "I've never seen a crowd like that. Not ever. It's great for Wales and great that people are feeling proud to be a Bluebird."

Fans make football, and fans made Cardiff City. They don't always follow the rules, but they're loud and they're loyal. During that 90 minutes, the fans didn't stop and rest, even for a second. Warnock added: "I'm proud that I've built a team capable of ruffling a few feathers. It's not quite sunk in yet, I've not had a drink yet, I daren't have one as I'll be drunk in two minutes!"

Joy can be won in football, not with pots of cash and rebrands, but with togetherness and tradition. Tradition: that tribal intangible defined by flag and dress and song and language and, most of all, history. Togetherness: a singular belief that our destiny is to be navigated as one.

Tan's rockstar treatment on that day was about the City faithful thanking him for finally understanding those things. When he spoke, after the party at the ground moved on to the capital's pubs and clubs, he showed a humility and generosity of spirit. Possibly enough to win back any remaining doubters.

This is a story of Warnock's Merlin-like magic touch, but it's also about Tan's own journey to truly recognising what it means to have the privilege of curating Cardiff City. His redemption, thanks to an education by the fans, was now complete. That was evident when he addressed the end of season awards, staged right after the Reading match at the Mercure Holland House Hotel in the city centre.

"First of all, I want to say thank you very much for giving me this opportunity to own a club that has seen good times and bad times," he said. "Thank you very much everyone. Who has done a better job than Neil Warnock? Today you can see that." An owner acknowledging to fans that they knew best? Tan, too, praising Warnock so emphatically was crucial. It was a sign that he understood there was more to the sum of City's promotion parts than luck and money.

That night, Morrison was awarded player of the season for his incredible performances and consistency and as the embodiment of the new, reborn Cardiff City. He thanked his teammates for "having my back", while he said Sol Bamba – who lost out on the trophy by 1% – was his own captain. "It's been incredible and today has been a day none of us will ever forget," he said.

He was right. Everybody – fan, player, director, steward, whoever else was there that Sunday afternoon – would always remember what they'd just been a part of. "There was a difference in that promotion, and I've seen a few now," adds Clive Rees. "There was an unexpectedness in this one, whereas with others there'd been higher hopes. This had been done against the odds and on a tight budget – we expected Aston Villa, or other teams who'd spent big, to be where we were, to go beyond us after our great start to the season. We kept the momentum going, right to the death, and that was a great achievement."

Warnock said: "I'm just so proud of them, that they listened to what I had to say. It seems such a long time ago [when I arrived at Cardiff], the state the club was in. I've seen the fans today on the pitch, a full house, the owners and everyone together, it's got to be the best ever job I've done in my life. We're going to get one or two things thrown at us next season, but hey ho, it's better than playing in the Championship."

True – but something much more had happened than a promotion. Dave Owens, a supporter since 1976 (he knows the date and game, Friday September 24, the day after his eighth birthday, when his brother took him to Ninian Park to watch City play Millwall), stopped watching City in 2012. He explains how the Wembley trips and play-off charges of the years before were an unknowing conclusion to a lifetime of supporting the Bluebirds. He thought he'd never come back.

"I'd dreamt my whole life of Cardiff City's ascension to the big time," Owens says. "I didn't realise, but it was the beginning of the end for me. When Peter Whittingham danced through the Teesiders' defence at the Riverside Stadium in the 2008 FA Cup quarter-final, the goal sent us into raptures as did the realisation that we were to play at Wembley for the first time since that famous FA Cup win over Arsenal in 1927.

"Despite the unbridled euphoria of Joe Ledley's volleyed goal in the semi-final to send us into dreamland – an appearance in the FA Cup Final, that London citadel was to be a wretched venue for the City.

"That first defeat against Portsmouth in the Cup final was easier to stomach because we were just glad to be participating in a game none of us could have ever imagined in our wildest flights of fancy back in those days of meagre pickings against the likes of Hartlepool and Stockport. Defeats in the play-off final against Blackpool and then Liverpool in the Carling Cup final were much harder to bear.

"Then in May 2012, almost four years to the day [we went up] came the bombshell. Vincent Tan's rebrand cut me off and cast me adrift from the football club that was once my abiding passion. That was it for me. No wavering, no hand-wringing, no indecision. I cut all ties immediately and vowed then I would never return."

Owens describes promotion to the Premier League in 2013 as a "hollow facsimile" of what should have been the greatest day in the club's history. "People asked me what it would take to bring me back. For me supporting Cardiff City was always about passion and identity. The Bluebirds were my club. Through good times and, let's face it, mainly bad, myself and those lifelong friends for whom supporting the City was much more than the football, would turn up to support our team, and it was that which ultimately led me to 'come home'."

In November 2016, Dave's best friend's dad died. "My brother may have taken me to my first match, but Mr H, as I called him, was the man who would ferry me, his son Andrew and a revolving cast of characters back and forth to Ninian Park in the '80s.

"In January 2017, two months after Mr H died and four and half years after I'd left the club behind, I came back. I figured it was what he would have wanted and his son was equally adamant it was what I should do. During the half-time interval in the 1-0 home victory against Aston Villa, the club paid tribute to him on the big screen and we all put on a flat cap and pulled out a half-time apple: his headwear and snack of choice. I knew then I would be back again – reunited with those lifelong friends with whom I shared so many brilliant memories."

Then came the next season – with Neil Warnock in charge and the club united as never before. "It was the right time. Time to move on, forgive and forget. I know Mr H would have been smiling down on all of us as the City achieved promotion to the Premier League. I don't recognise Cardiff City's brief tenure in the top flight. It wasn't my club, but this coming season means so much to all of us for so many reasons – and most of them have nothing to do with football. Friendship, camaraderie and community will endure – whatever happens on the pitch."

11

Forward Cardiff

"I think we have got a group of lads who can surprise a few. We've got the lowest budget, almost by a half, but that doesn't bother me. I spoke to Vincent and told him I'm not bothered about that at all."

Neil Warnock

Football can save us from ourselves. When Brexit was all anyone wanted (or didn't want, but found it impossible not to) talk about, football saved us from everyone else, too. Or at least for a moment.

As the Tory government teetered from crisis to catastrophe, with chief Brexiteers Boris Johnson and David Davis resigning, and the population decamped to the beach until the heatwave broke, one of the most memorable World Cups was happening in Russia, and Cardiff lad Geraint Thomas became the first Welshman to win the *Tour de France*.

Cardiff City also did some very un-Cardiff City things. Summer 2018, for the Bluebirds, was about preparing for the Premier League, not only with the purpose to stay there, but also with the determination to secure a future. Security is no synonym for Cardiff City with its history of High Court hearings and winding-up orders. It's definitely not been a place to come to see a business with its house in order.

In the immediate aftermath of the season's end, Vincent Tan was continuing his reconciliation with supporters. He'd admitted his mistakes and promised "no more tinkering". He wanted to make the club "bigger, stronger, better, greater" together with the supporters. He'd bought into Team Warnock and his idea that everyone was part of the first team project.

Tan promised a new kind of Cardiff City to the one promoted five years ago. It would be a City of prudence and sense. There'd be no extravagant money spent on big name players because that was the old way of doing things. Just look, he said, at what Leicester had achieved buying Jamie Vardy for £1m and Riyad Mahrez for £450,000 (no pressure, Neil but if you can win the Premier League on a shoestring, then that'd be great).

Tan reaffirmed his commitment to Cardiff, he didn't want to sell up and leave unless someone came to him with a ridiculous offer – £500m would do – and would be backing Neil Warnock whatever. Oh, and he absolutely, 100%, was never ever going to change the club colours, ever again. Lesson most definitely learned on that one.

If Tan wanted City to do a Leicester, then Warnock was a bit more measured about top flight prospects. "I think we'll be OK," he told me, a few weeks before pre-season training began. A classic Yorkshire understatement, but why give fans false expectations? His excitement at being given the proper crack at the Premier League he'd always wanted was plain, but there was no way Warnock would promise the unachievable.

"A small element will be expecting us to be in Europe!" he joked, but, says Warnock, the situation is "unique". Cardiff have overachieved, unlike many promotion trailblazers before them. "I think we have got a group of lads who can surprise a few. We've got the lowest budget, almost by a half, but that doesn't bother me. I spoke to Vincent and told him I'm not bothered about that at all. If the recruitment carries on like it is then I'll be happy. The first two we brought in were my main two and if I can get three or four other lads that we want, I think we'll be OK."

His budget for the season was dwarfed by every other club, even that of Huddersfield's – a much smaller club than City. He wasn't afraid to say that, and he was far from ashamed of that fact either. For the Yorkshireman, the Premier League adventure with Cardiff City was going to be as much about proving a point, as the season before had been. He was going to give it a go and give it a go his way: picking up the right players and paying the right price.

Warnock likes to do his business as early in the close season as possible. It gives his squad a better chance to bond. He can also gauge properly the kind of character that squad has. Remember the barbecue at his home before the last season? That's when he knew the season ahead would be magic.

To that end, the summer of 2018 was not one of revolution, nor did it have shock exits or galactico arrivals. This was for building on the Warnock-masterminded transformation, long-termism as well as ensuring recruits fitted into a squad which had clicked so well.

First in was Josh Murphy. Perhaps, knowing how much Warnock loves wingers (as a former wide man himself), his first Premier League recruit for the Bluebirds was one full of pace and promise. The fee was believed to be around £11m, not much in 2018 for a Premier League forward – but that's exactly what Vincent Tan was demanding in the summer's recruitment drive.

A day later, Greg Cunningham, a player Warnock had apparently been chasing since he arrived at Cardiff, joined from

Preston. The left-back was added to provide competition for Joe Bennett. Considering Warnock had told fans at the end of season awards that Bennett was as good a full-back as he'd ever worked with in his career, Cunningham was bound to be a fine acquisition.

City's signings were coming in pairs. Bobby Reid, Bristol City's highly-rated forward, was signed for around £10m and Alex Smithies, the goalkeeper, joined from QPR for about £4m to provide healthy competition for Neil Etheridge.

These deals were done well before the pre-season fixtures were underway, before even pre-season training. It looked like Warnock's most wanted men were joining first. He admitted as much. His knowledge of the Championship and eye for a player with potential was being used differently now, these were players he'd been watching for a few years, players he believed could do a job at the top level and players he thought would be sought after by bigger clubs after they'd been given their chance by Cardiff.

It was a different approach from the last time City were in the Premier League, when the summer transfer window had plenty of impressive signings, which arguably hurt the dynamic of the squad. This time, Warnock knew who he trusted and knew what he wanted to add.

Warnock had just flown to Malaysia for a transfer and budget summit with owner Vincent Tan. The pair discussed finances and targets for the months ahead. There were to be no surprises for the manager as he got ready for another massive season to come. He knew exactly what was expected of him and what could be expected from his employer. Clarity is all Warnock wants – and he loves making a success of things without the resources others are afforded.

As Warnock was spending relative pennies in the Premier League, the other promoted clubs – Wolves and Fulham – were paying tens of millions for international stars. Warnock told *WalesOnline* in June: "Vincent Tan, I spoke to him about the wage bill. I knew the wage bill was going to be probably lower than most of them in the Premier League but that doesn't bother me at all. I enjoyed my conversations with Vincent. I just said I'm trying to get value for money. He's supported me, with Mehmet Dalman and Ken Choo."

As important as the new signings were, the way the club rewarded players who'd been a part of the promotion project was refreshing and positive. With the summer heat drawing on, there was a drip, drip, drip of good news coming from the club, and by the beginning of July, new contracts had been signed by several players, while the future of others had also been decided.

Ever since May and the promotion parade, there was a growing concern that Junior Hoilett, voted players' player of the season, would not be signing a new deal. He was out of contract and yet, despite hinting he wanted to stay, had not done the important thing of putting pen to paper. One wonders what was keeping him, but eventually, on June 26, Hoilett signed a three-year contract, saying how "amazing" it felt to be committing himself to the club. Phew! You could hear the sighs of relief across Cardiff.

"It was always going to happen though: I want to continue my career here and never wanted to go anywhere else," Hoilett told the official website. "I want to go on and achieve more things in the Premier League with a great group of lads. The fans have supported me so much since I've been here. I have so much respect for them and it was a no-brainer to stay here and continue that great relationship."

A no-brainer which just left Aron Gunnarsson, the other outstanding out-of-contract player, to sign with the club. He had the small matter of captaining his country at the World

Cup to get out of the way first. Then, a couple of months after the end of the season, Warnock revealed we needn't have been worried all along – Gunnarsson had told him during the summer that he wanted in.

Warnock told everyone about Gunnarsson's City commitment when a load of other players had been awarded extensions or new deals. Joe Bennett was first to go public with his new contract on July 3. Then came Nathaniel Mendez-Laing, Sean Morrison, Callum Paterson, Joe Ralls, Sean Morrison, Lee Peltier and Matthew Connolly. This wasn't the traditional Cardiff City way of doing business.

Contracts are supposed to be run down to the wire and leave players and fans in a state of uncertainty over the future. Instead, in a hitherto unprecedented move of forward thinking, a raft of first-teamers had been shown loyalty for their own immense commitment. Some of them had stuck with the club through some really tough times, and now they were going to be a part of the Cardiff City Premier League project.

That Matthew Connolly, who many City fans would not have anywhere near the first team, was given a two-year deal, illustrated the Warnock managerial methodology incredibly well. Connolly had endured some recent, difficult injury-punctuated seasons, but Warnock was putting his faith in him.

At the player of the year awards, he described Connolly as an "unsung hero" who he'd "play tomorrow if I had to". He'd said something similar the year before. Fans may not see it, but Connolly is certainly a manager's player and was rewarded for it.

With all those players signing new contracts, Warnock spoke of Iceland captain Gunnarsson's future: "Aron wanted to repay the club, and Vincent, for the support he's had here over the past seven years. He wants to help us try and stay in the Premier

League, and I think that's great. We had a chat six weeks ago [ahead of the World Cup] and he told me he wanted to stay; now we're looking forward to him coming back in to the group."

Crucially, Ralls (probably one of the more saleable assets in the squad, given his age and potential) was tied in long-term, it was a tantalising prospect to see how he'd do in the Premier League. There was similar reason to anticipate the spectre of Paterson and Mendez-Laing, with all their raw ability, playing against the country's top teams.

A few days later it was formally done and Gunnarsson had signed a new one-year contract. Not perfect, but preferable to seeing such a popular and important player leave before having another go at the Premier League with Cardiff.

"I always wanted to stay and I told the gaffer that," said Gunnarsson. "Even though I didn't say much in the news, I just wanted to do my job on the pitch. It was tough work to get back, ready to represent my country at the World Cup, and for Cardiff City. Now, signing this deal has been my number one priority and I can't wait to meet back up with the boys. My little boy was born in Cardiff and I've been through a lot with this club and the fans."

Quotes to get fans drooling over, that's for sure. The players were even breaking through the football cliché barrier and speaking with integrity. Gunnarsson had been there with us through all the rubbish, he felt the pain too. Now he was going to enjoy some good times.

"We've done brilliantly," Warnock beamed as the signings were announced. They were as important as adding new talent – because they gave the playing side of the club stability and a spine. They ensured the Neil Warnock Cardiff City Way would endure, probably, beyond his stay at the club. If Warnock often has an eye only for the here and now, this was him ticking the long-term boxes too.

Tan talked about acting on Warnock's advice on the under-23s, making sure the youth project provides talent for the first team. The long-term deals ensured there'd be no Joe Ledley or Adam Matthews-style departures on free transfers or tribunal-set fees. It was good business.

Even the departure of players was dignified. Utility player Greg Halford, who'd been training with the club despite not being given a new contract, announced he was leaving. His statement lamented the fact that "everything comes to an end eventually". He described the squad as "the best group of lads I've worked with", and said he'd "made friends for life here". He thanked the chief executive, the chairman, the coaching team and Warnock and said he "hoped to repay them at some point in the future". Then, of course, he thanked the fans who had made his City stay so memorable. Another club insider eulogising eloquently on his exit about the unity at Cardiff City.

Instability and controversy continued across the UK, with the visit of Donald Trump in July, and more Brexit shenanigans. Football, if your team was Cardiff, was providing more comfort and security.

Important statements were being made about players and investment in the squad, about the direction the football policy was being taken. There was a longer-term vision now, rather than the necessary quick fix of stopping relegation and winning promotion in the space of less than 18 months.

Something hugely important was also going on at boardroom level. Vincent Tan was clearing the massive debt the club owed him. Bit by bit, he was doing something no previous owner had: thinking about a legacy and making sure there would be a Cardiff City for years to come.

In a press release full of business-speak, it was announced that Tan had made a hugely significant financial commitment.

By the end of May, the press office revealed Tan had converted almost £70m-worth of loans he'd made to the club into equity. It meant the club's debt to him now stood at £50m – still massive, but dwarfed by the £115m he was owed before, and he'd already converted £12.6m from debt into equity during the previous 12 months.

The Cardiff City Supporters' Trust, which has criticised Tan's handling of the ownership reins in previous years, now gave an unequivocal message of support to what he was doing. Keith Morgan, the trust's chairman, said: "Firstly, there has been a further massive conversion of debt, due to the owner Vincent Tan, into equity (shares). The amount involved is a huge £66.4m and is in addition to conversions of £8m in an earlier year and £12.7m in June 2017. This is a major boost to the club's balance sheet position and is a further great example of Vincent Tan's continued commitment to the club."

Crucially, the club was also compliant with financial fair play rules – an "encouraging" step, added Morgan. Shrewd, generous, prudent. City were worthy of all those adjectives in the way they were going about business. For fans, it was the perfect summer.

Supporter Phil Nifield said: "I think fans want the club to spend sensibly now we're back in the Premier League. I think the unity is the thing and there's a danger that if you bring in big stars, there won't be the same unity. Warnock is pretty shrewd. I didn't enjoy it at all the last time we were in the Premier League, because of the rebrand and the business between Vincent Tan and Malky Mackay. We will lose a lot more than we will win next season but hopefully we'll do enough to stay up. He'll give it a good go and I hope they stick with him. Things will get difficult at times."

James Leighton, however, was looking beyond the next season. "I'm pretty certain we're going to be on the end of some right hammerings, but whatever happens, Neil Warnock deserves his opportunity to leave the club when he wants to, because God knows where we would be had he not come in. If we do go down I just think this has really rebuilt the club and set the foundations for the future."

Warnock was also keen to see how his signings would do in the top division, saying they might be talked about "going to the very top" when the season was done. He clearly had ambitions for the club to do well, but also to see his gift for talent spotting bearing fruit again – £10m may be a lot to spend on a player in the history of Cardiff City, but in the context of the mega wealth at the top of the English game, it's a snip for a Premier League club.

Speaking as his squad came back for pre-season, he said: "Alex Smithies is great for competition with Neil [Etheridge], he's a smashing lad. You've got Greg Cunningham and we had to have another left-sided lad. Joe Bennett's done well and Greg's in to give him more competition, and he can play centre-half as well.

"Then your strikers, when I look at Bobby Reid and Josh Murphy, they give us something added. That's what you pay for, I suppose. Everybody says they're untried, but you've got to start somewhere. You can see how hungry they are in the training sessions."

Promotion precipitated a new long-termism at the club, and Cardiff as a capital city stood to benefit.

You might not be able to measure exactly what it means for the club to be promoted, but in many ways that doesn't matter. In fact, economically, it probably doesn't make much difference at all to the city's wealth, but a place in the Premier League was vitally important to the club's finances. Without it the club would have had to find a way of plugging a £20m shortfall, according to the supporters trust. Parachute payments would have now run out and the club would be losing money and struggling in the lower reaches of the Championship. That's how much Warnock's promotion meant to the leadership at Leckwith.

Let's tie down the players long-term and look further ahead to the future, with a broader view of Cardiff City Football Club. As Morgan acknowledges, the city can enjoy a kudos associated with having a team playing in one of the world's most glamorous and watched leagues.

Revealing the huge impact on Cardiff when it staged the Champions League final – £45m added to the region's economy by the match in May 2017 – Huw Thomas, Cardiff Council's leader, said he hoped for a ripple effect. "It was unbelievable and that effect is carrying on and will get even bigger with Cardiff City in the Premier League," he said. "We've seen some record numbers of visitors coming to Cardiff. We saw around 20 million visit last year [2017] which is a record. It's useful having that name recognition which is important when you're having meetings around the world about selling Cardiff as a visitor destination."

We're told footballers have a blinkered sense of the world – understanding what they must do on a Saturday but little else. In reality, as people who decamp to the area from around the UK and the globe, they become tuned into the place where they earn their living. City's players obviously feel emotional about what they've done for fans in Cardiff.

With a manager like Warnock, it would be hard for them to ignore what's going on around them and the impact their success could have on local communities. Warnock's pre-season ritual gathering in Cornwall was preceded by another friendly at Taff's Well, a couple of days after England were knocked out of the World Cup – and, as City fans joked, the game where football really did come home. The result didn't matter. The Bluebirds knew it would be a victory: it was 3-0 in the end. More important than even the practice for the players (this time Warnock used it to give the under-23s a runout and have a look at some young trialists), was the fact that money was again raised for charity. The first team were there, despite not playing, meeting supporters, signing autographs and having their pictures taken with fans.

Warnock took to the microphone before the match to tell fans, again, of his expectation that his side would be "ruffling feathers" the following season. "It's nice to see all the lads here signing autographs and I'm sure you'll see them perform in Cornwall next week. It's a lovely occasion and we've got some good young lads playing here tonight," he said.

Warnock told me he's glad he's not been pushed into taking his side on a headline-grabbing tour of China, Thailand or Malaysia. He cherishes the routine he's established and for this special Premier League preparation year, a few extra games were added so a larger squad of players could enjoy the benefits of the expedition to Cornwall.

The friendly fixtures read like a glossary of clubs from Warnock's autobiography – along with the usual local teams near his Cornwall home, there was ex-club Torquay as well as Rotherham and Burton, both of which he played for and managed.

Nothing much different about this pre-season from Warnock's point of view, then. He still wanted the players to use this time to appreciate the fans who follow them, before the intensity begins. They may now be Premier League, but they need to know their place.

Whatever's to happen in City's return to the top division, whether a relegation dog-fight or a shock top-six finish, whether Warnock stays or he goes, there's everything to be hopeful about in the future.

"Neil Warnock is without doubt the best manager we've ever had," says long-time fan Clive Rees. "He took over from Paul Trollope at a time which I think was probably the low point. There was more entertainment talking to people around you than watching a game. Warnock was brought in and got us out of the relegation fight and then, amazingly, won promotion.

"Now he's signing the right calibre of player, I think, for the Premier League and characters who will fit into a Neil Warnock team. People say he's not a top flight manager and whatever club he's been at have been favourites for relegation, but I think it's different this time, he's had more time at the club and he's already built solid foundations.

"With the budget he has, he's brought in hot prospects from the Championship who could become even better players. The essence of the players he's signed are young, hungry players with a point to prove rather than experienced Premier League players who've been around and who'd come for a fat salary and signing-on fee. I'm excited about our chances. I think we have a chance in the mini-league we'll be competing in alongside the likes of Brighton and Huddersfield, because that's where our fate will be decided. We're starting a season with stability, and we really haven't had that for many years."

Gordon Goldsmith, who's been supporting City since 1966, is also excited. "It won't be easy but when things start to get tough, the fans will stick by the team," he said. "It seems to be the best the club has ever been run, and that's a great start. I'm optimistic. I think Warnock is so refreshing – he's honest, realistic and he's down-to-earth. I think he's a fantastic person and I'm so glad he's won the fans back. He could almost be a stand-up comedian – although he might not be to everyone's taste. I've never felt this positive about Cardiff City."

Another Bluebird fan, Siân Matheson, says the "genuine feeling of togetherness" makes this stint in the top flight different. "We know it's not going to be pretty at times, but if the boys give their all on the pitch, anything can happen. As long as our warrior-leader Neil Warnock stays at the helm, I think we stand every chance of survival – and are more than capable of achieving a few shock results. Bring it on!"

After decades of desperation, a new Cardiff City is emerging, whatever the Bluebirds' destiny in the Premier League come May, 2019.

Afterword

From Sloper Road to the Premier League

I well remember the sights, sounds, smells and emotions as a kid going down the match with my dad. As we drove over the brow of the hill from Ely Bridge, dropping down to Cowbridge Road East, we'd see our first glimpse of Ninian Park's impressive floodlights, spiking out of the terraced streets of Canton and Grangetown. Dad, smoking a Hamlet cigar ("Don't tell your mother!"), would take our Austin Montego to Broad Street where we'd park up, half an hour to kick-off, before a five minute walk to the old ground. Dad would tell stories of him and Grancha coming down years before, of watching the City in Division One when the place was bursting at the seams ("Full? Wow!"). Names from eras past: Derek Tapscott, Trevor Ford, Brian Clark and Don Murray were drilled into my memory as though I'd seen them play myself.

From the moment I saw those towering lights, the excitement in my belly would burn. Dad would buy us a programme from the same seller on Sloper Road, we'd part company at the turnstiles, tut if there was a queue ("Where were these fans every other week?"), drink sweet, black coffee from Dad's flask, read every page of the programme from front to back, intently watch the City players go through their warm-ups. Then the match: mesmerising, exciting, absorbing. Even in Division Four.

We wouldn't miss a kick, finding joy in the most dour of games. Then home: a stop off at the newsagents under the bridge in Fairwater to collect a *Football Echo* (if City had won) and back in time to see the first half goal (if there was one) on HTV news.

Age might dull the anticipation a little, but the same childish excitement never really wears off. It's why the most placid of adults can turn salivating barbarian once the referee's whistle blows. The Saturday ritual has changed down the years, family, work, adulthood eat into it and you lose some of the innocent sense of wonder. The new ground is missing four great pylons, but the passion for the Bluebirds is as strong as it ever was.

There was a hiatus from that. Not long ago. There was for many. Going down the City was still something we did, but it was less an hour-and-a-half of intense emotion you couldn't live without, and more a chance to catch up with others – the friends and relatives we went with and were used to seeing every other week.

Cardiff City was losing touch with us. We still went. We still wanted the club to do well, but something had happened, something had come between us and it just wasn't the same. We have one man to thank for salvaging the passion. For making us *want* to go to see Cardiff City play, rather than the sense of *having* to go.

In decades to come we might remember, fondly, the promotion season of 2017-18. That's the thing that'll be recorded forever in the club's honours list – and rightly so.

The abiding motif which has emerged from the many conversations I've had with people over the last few months, is that the greatest legacy of the 2017-18 season is the reunification of the club. Its rebirth. It's been a constant theme through everything I've written.

Before Neil Warnock came, and even after the colours were reverted to blue, fans were like family members who'd fallen out and refused to speak. There was no togetherness, no connection between players and supporters. The atmosphere was flat and attendances were drifting away. His counselling work has helped us rediscover what Cardiff City meant to many of us, for others it prompted their first steps back through the Cardiff City Stadium turnstiles after years away. Winning has been the ultimate carrot to lure the drifters back, but it's been about so much more than that. I don't think there will be another season like the one we had in 2017-18. It needed the despair of the previous years to make it so thrilling. It was the vent which cleared mind and spirit. That the team played the football that it did made it all the more appropriate.

People talk about blood and thunder, commitment, and never giving up. The squad had these characteristics in abundance. It more than made up for matches lacking spark.

There was also something, as I wrote these pages, to emerge from the World Cup – something like validation, for the style of play City have adopted under Warnock. Teams were not afraid to cede play to the opposition, set pieces were important means of scoring goals. France won the tournament in a game where they enjoyed just 34% possession of the ball. The 'long ball game' was back in fashion.

Cardiff's manager was actually at the vanguard of change. It might not be pretty all of the time, but it's damned effective. It'll win you games, it'll get you up. Because, even after (an eighth) promotion, for some reason it feels like Neil Warnock's style of play, style of winning, needs vindication. It doesn't to Cardiff fans who've loved every minute of Warnock's "roller coaster".

Now the Bluebirds are back in the Premier League. It might end up being another one-season stay, it may be the beginning of a new, and long-awaited for, top flight era. Either way, a legacy has been secured. If the manager is the most important position at a football club, then Warnock has lived up to every expectation and beyond.

Is there anyone in any other decade, let alone this one, who could have done what Warnock has achieved? Arguably not. It's easy to get carried away with his singular impact on the club, for he has his henchmen – Ronnie Jepson and Kevin Blackwell – while Vincent Tan, Mehmet Dalman and Ken Choo have all contributed to his joining and his staying. The change has been down to Warnock, but he is ever a team man, he talks of "we" and "us" (and definitely never in the royal sense) when you ask him about the job he's done at Cardiff. This is a team effort, the rebuilding of Cardiff City may have been masterminded by Warnock, but it was delivered by everyone at the club. Especially the fans – for we'd fallen in love with football again, and we'd fallen back in love with Cardiff City.

ST DAVID'S PRESS

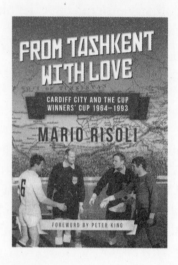

'an enjoyable and emotional read'
Peter King, Cardiff City FC 1960-1974

'a great tribute to a glorious time'
Jeremy Bowen, award-winning Journalist

From Tashkent With Love is a tale of courage, heartbreak and glory spanning four decades. It tells the remarkable story of Cardiff City's football adventures across Europe in the European Cup Winners' Cup.

From the thrilling 1-0 victory against the mighty Real Madrid at Ninian Park in 1971, to the heartbreak of a last minute 3-2 home defeat in the semi-final against FC Hamburg in 1968, Cardiff's 24 Cup Winners' Cup games are all recalled by the best-selling author Mario Risoli who interviewed over 70 former players in the writing of this comprehensive book.

Their 29-year European odyssey saw the Bluebirds face some of the biggest names in continental football - Sporting Lisbon, Zaragoza, FC Porto and Dynamo Berlin - and included their epic 1968 pulsating quarter-final tie against the crack Soviet side Torpedo Moscow. With the game switched from icy Moscow to Tashkent, in what is now Uzbekistan, City were forced to make a remarkable 8,000-mile round trip to the borderlands of China and Afghanistan, a journey which still survives as one of the furthest distances travelled by any British club in a European cup competition.

pb - 978 1 902719 412 - £16.99 - 384pp + 40pp of photographs